WOVEN
&
WORN

CANOPY PRESS

First published in the United Kingdom, 2019, by Canopy Press.
An imprint of 3dtotal Publishing.

Address: 3dtotal.com Ltd, 29 Foregate Street, Worcester, WR1 1DS, United Kingdom.

Correspondence: publishing@3dtotal.com

Website: www.canopy-press.com

ISBN: 978-1-909414-91-4

Printing and binding: Gomer Press, UK
www.gomer.co.uk

Visit www.canopy-press.com for a complete list of available book titles.

Managing Director: Tom Greenway
Studio Manager: Simon Morse
Assistant Manager: Melanie Robinson
Lead Designer: Imogen Williams
Publishing Manager: Jenny Fox-Proverbs
Designer: Joseph Cartwright
Editor: Sophie Symes
Illustrations: Marisa Lewis

FSC
www.fsc.org
MIX
Paper from responsible sources
FSC® C114687

Back cover photographs (from top to bottom): ©Roke, © Karen Pearson, © Miquel Llonch

"Clothing connects people around the world; however different our traditions may be, we all wear clothes, and feel that they represent us"

Paola Masperi, Mayamiko

CANOPY PRESS

An imprint of 3dtotal Publishing, Canopy Press was established in 2018 to create books focused on traditional crafts, lifestyle, and the environment. With an interest in enjoying the simple things in life, Canopy Press aims to build awareness around sustainable living, a mindful approach to arts and crafts, and an appreciation of the earth we dwell on.

Marrying great aesthetics with enlightening stories from real people, our *Search for Well-being and Sustainability in the Modern World* series presents an insight into heritage crafts and artisan food, and their revival and survival in the modern world. Visit our website and follow us on Instagram to stay up to date with forthcoming books and news.

canopy-press.com | instagram.com/canopypress

CONTENTS

FOREWORD

Patrick McDowell
Sustainable Fashion Designer and Creative Education Advocate

We are at a turning point in fashion; our relatively young industry is leaving its terrible twos behind and embarking on a more conscientious future. The global growth of brands with ethical and positive mission statements tells us that there is a hunger for clothing that doesn't cost the earth.

Sustainability holds the power to redesign all aspects of the fashion industry; from design to retail, and crucially how we experience and think of clothes. If we consider ourselves as citizens rather than consumers, making decisions through our clothes will stay true to our values. As Orsola De Castro, Co-Founder of Fashion Revolution once said, "If you own clothes, you are part of the fashion supply chain", and as part of the chain, we therefore all have an opportunity to initiate a positive change. When investing in sustainable fashion there is an extra level of emotion; knowing the person who made your clothing was fairly treated and paid, and that the fabric is not polluting the planet while still looking good, feels incredible.

> "The global growth of brands with ethical and positive mission statements tells us that there is a hunger for clothing that doesn't cost the earth"

Fashion has a wonderful ability to tell others so much about us, and more importantly it can make you feel confident and enable you to do things you wouldn't have thought you could. This is the reason I started designing clothing – being a part of those personal moments through clothing is so special and beautiful. Although in its basic function clothing protects and insulates us, in reality it offers so much more. Back when I was in school, aged thirteen, the only part of my uniform that wasn't controlled was my bag, and because of this (and the fact that my parents refused to buy me a new one) I started sewing and made a satchel using just an old pair of jeans and a needle and thread. The need to express one's self through the clothes and decorations you wear is present in every culture.

Often it is through challenging moments like those I faced at school that real creativity becomes apparent. Designing sustainably offers those same challenges and moments of ingenuity. It forces you to work around your limitations and come up with creative solutions, in turn offering a more enticing, creative future for industries across the globe.

I create design-led sustainable garments, that don't compromise on aesthetic or experience; they in fact enhance both. When I design, I have a whole host of extra elements to think about. I see these as design challenges that will eventually make the final product more desirable. Using reclaimed materials means that quantities of my products are limited and I can't simply go and buy more. I find myself going into a second design stage where I look at my sketch and the materials I have and find the best way for them to work together. In the same way, I take apart pieces from my last collection to use the fabric in the next; engaging with circularity and redesigning luxury. The fabrics are then so limited that it makes each piece extra special, with an additonal layer and story, and in some cases, a very limited period of time where it actually exists.

> "I create design-led sustainable garments, that don't compromise on aesthetic or experience; they in fact enhance both"

It is important to remember that the world of sustainability is full of new and exciting ways of working and experiencing fashion, as many of the makers featured in this book are already demonstrating. One of the most wonderful aspects of sustainability is that we see a return to the craft of clothing. For a number of years, we lost sight of the processes involved in creating; the weaving, pattern cutting and dressmaking were often hidden away. Increasingly we are celebrating these fundamental steps to producing a well-rounded garment and they are increasingly engaged with by new designers who want to not only design beautiful clothes but also to understand the crafts that allow them to happen.

As we move forward, the world of sustainability will expand and eventually the name will slip away as we come to expect higher standards: the correct treatment of those in supply chains, the use of non-harmful materials and a respect for craft. However, in the meantime the change starts with you.

INTRODUCTION

Arianna Nicoletti
Circular Fashion Expert and Sustainable Innovation Advocate

A CREATIVE FUTURE

We are witnessing a radical change within the fashion industry, for the positive. If the past fifty years have been marked by the establishment of the so-called "Fast Fashion" system, this last decade saw the parallel rising of a global sustainable fashion movement that is radically re-shaping the industrial landscape. Sustainability is no longer limited to pilot projects and tenacious change makers. Brands of any size now have the opportunity to create sustainable and transparent supply chains on a global scale. At the same time, people from all around the world are awakening from their passive attitude towards clothes and textile consumption. Consumers are starting to resolutely ask for more transparency and better working conditions within the fashion industry. A multitude of different platforms, from online information sites, to global campaigns and social media activities, are supporting consumers in raising their voice and showing their economic power.

At a time in which almost every daily life interaction is digitalised and culture is globalised, the importance of maintaining contact with our own traditions and "know-hows" is invaluable. Re-learning maker skills is an essential step for our society towards a new harmonisation with human values linked to the making of textiles and clothing. Looking closer at the work of modern artisans, at their inclusive way of doing business as well as at their challenges, is key to start re-evaluating our relationship to clothes, materials, and the beauty of making.

> "In a time in which almost every daily life interaction is digitalised and culture is globalised, the importance of maintaining contact with our own traditions and "know-hows" is invaluable"

THE LINEAR FASHION SYSTEM:
SOME IMPORTANT FACTS

The average lifespan of a garment is only 3 years in western countries. Compared to 20 years ago, consumers globally keep clothes about half the time they used to. Between 2000 and 2015 this time decreased to a third, due to the poor quality of textiles, and the fast-shifting trends and styles. [1]

Around 75% of all used or unsold garments end up landfilled or incinerated worldwide. According to the Ellen McArthur Foundation currently only 1% of material used to produce clothing is recycled into new clothing. [2]

More than 50% of fast fashion items produced are disposed of in less than a year. The United States Environmental Protection Agency states that 12.8 million tonnes of textiles are landfilled every year. [3]

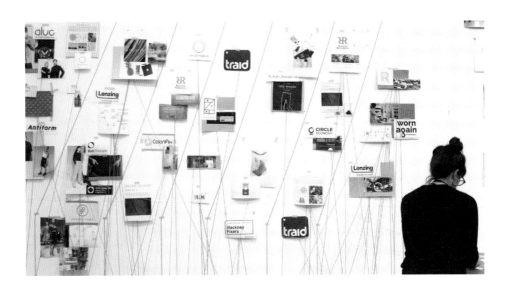

In the current linear production system, garments are not designed to reduce waste, instead inefficient design and production processes generate huge volumes of leftovers. The software platform *Reverse Resources* estimates that an average of 25% of resources are lost for various reasons along the fashion supply chain. The generation of these leftovers can reach up to 47% of the total amount of fibres and textiles bought by a factory. [4]

The production of textile waste is not limited to the leftovers from materials or semi-finished products. In fact, immense quantities of brand-new garments are landfilled or incinerated due to the global overproduction of fashion items. It is estimated that around 30% of all the clothes we produce remain unsold.[5]

In order to be efficiently recycled and to obtain a higher quality of recycling fibres, leftover and second-hand textiles should be sorted according to their fibre composition. The scarce traceability of the textile material content makes it incredibly hard to set up efficient recycling systems.

Synthetic textiles such as polyester are one of the main sources of microplastic pollution and account for 35% of all microplastics. About 2,000 synthetic particles are released from washing a single polyester fleece jacket, with huge consequences for our environment.[6]

POWER TO THE CONSUMER

As users/consumers, we assume that we are the very last link in the fashion value chain. Contrariwise, we are just in the middle of it. Considering the global extent of our consumption, our decisions in terms of buying, using, and discarding of clothing critically affects the world we live in. The incredibly low prices of garments, together with the increasing speed of changing trends and questionable quality of materials, tell us a story of throwaway clothes that can be easily disposed of. Disconnected from human value, shopping becomes compulsive, addictive, as well as necessary to fulfil our sense of belonging to the community.

> "... we consume fashion 400 times more than we did twenty years ago"

These uncontrolled consumption patterns are the result of decades of fast-fashion culture, aiming to maximize economic profits at the cost of human and environmental welfare. Making us passive consumers, this system was able to cover with a glossy layer, the inconvenient truth: shocking working conditions in production countries, uncontrolled use of hazardous chemicals, pollution and the absurd abuse of natural resources.

According to the documentary *The True Cost*, today we consume fashion 400 times more than we did twenty years ago. Meanwhile, the average life of a garment in our wardrobes sank to only seven wears per piece. Mountains of inexpensive – almost unworn! – clothes pile up and eventually get discarded at such a high volume that neither charities nor recyclers are able to manage in an efficient way. Every year 92 million tonnes of textile waste ends up in landfills or is incinerated across the globe. It is clear that without a change in our consumption patterns there cannot be any form of radical transformation within the industry. The good news is: there are plenty of alternatives and strategies out there to support us in becoming conscious consumers and ethical influencers.

We are living in the era of participatory consumption. Thanks to the digitalisation of communication and sales processes, consumers have become co-designers, customisers and decision-makers. The concept of ownership has changed too. A huge number of online platforms, apps and web shops are establishing sharing economy models for the fashion sector – leasing, borrowing, re-selling, and swapping are becoming common practice with the youngest fashion consumers. At the same time, buying criteria, such as material quality or uniqueness of style are growing in importance. Consuming for decades within a system based on the replication of designs, produced in vast quantities without distinction of provenance, we are striving for originality and creativity. *Grove & Co.* is an example of a design approach based on exclusivity. Understanding the current relevance of individuality in fashion, the two founders create a unique series of shirts using industrial leftover fabrics.

More and more fashion brands now apply innovative circularity strategies such as zero-waste pattern cutting or material upcycling at the design stage, in order to reduce the use of virgin resources. The Spanish label *Demano* is a perfect example of the smart use of unwanted materials to make one of a kind accessories. The banners, kite sails, and old umbrellas used for these creations are sourced locally and are repurposed in products carrying a beautiful story.

"Upcycling" is a smart development of the word "recycling" that shows us how a material value can actually be *upgraded* through the process of design. It is a term that acknowledges that simply through the application of human skills we are able to transform the perceived emotional and financial worth of clothes. This is the magic behind handicrafts that our society is rediscovering.

Social media channels make it possible for brands to share their stories and philosophies in a very intimate way. Consumers can inform themselves and actively ask the labels about their transparency. Sustainable fashion is riding the wave of media success and the shopping experience, even if digital, starts to be perceived once more as a moment of human interaction with designers and makers.

FUTURE MATERIALS

We are living in a time in which technological innovation plays an important role in every production and service sector. In the field of fashion, we are experiencing an escalation of cutting-edge industrial developments applying synthetic biotechnologies to textiles.

Researching the topic of "the future of fashion" last year during my residency at the Victoria and Albert Museum in London, I initially believed these new technologies would increase the potential for circularity and sustainability in fashion. Using organic components, such as bacteria or proteins, synthetic biology aims to create biological materials that do not already exist in the natural world.

> "We are living in a time in which technological innovation plays an important role in every production and service sector"

Translated into fashion, it is possible to use organic elements to grow materials and fibres, such as "mushroom leather" or "spider silk". These alternative materials can be generated in closed-loop systems, usually through fermentation processes of completely renewable inputs. Beside this, through the bioengineering of the organic components, desirable attributes of the fibre can be fine-tuned in a laboratory; including resilience, elasticity and colour – reducing the need for chemical applications and consequently leading to a higher biodegradability of textiles.

These are immense achievements and should the fashion industry continue to develop hand in hand with synthetic biology, we could see the production of sustainable materials on a larger scale in the near future. However: "Can biology do it better?". Dr Daisy Ginsberg and Audrey Natsai Chieza, UK-based researchers on the matter, ask themselves this question in an article titled, "Other Biological Futures". If these technologies keep working within the same financial and consumption frameworks of the fast fashion industry, where is their real potential for change? In fact, the risk is that "we may simply shift reliance from petrochemicals to other carbon-based feedstocks like sugar for the production of materials", so says Ginsberg and Chieza. Technologies, in order to be disruptive, need to find their social and political dimension to change the system they work within.

At this point in my research I started considering other potential avenues for future change, and started looking more closely at materials and practices that were actually traditional for local societies in the past. One example was particularly inspiring: natural dyer Sachio Yoshioka. When Sachio inherited the four-generation family businesses in 1988, he decided to move from synthetic dyes to the exclusive use of natural inputs. In an interview filmed by the V&A in his workshop in Kyoto he says: "The colors you can obtain from plants are so beautiful. This is the reason I do what I do.".

Natural fibres and plant-based colours are seeing a renaissance. Innumerable Instagram feeds and dedicated blogs, featuring aesthetically perfect images of small textiles swatches dyed with different seeds, indigo plants, gardens or minced colourful roots and flowers ready to be used, demonstrate that younger generations are rediscovering the beauty of these traditional techniques. Communities of urban crafters are popping up on every corner of the planet to meet and share their regained knowledge. These contemporary artisans are developing a brand-new connection to human skills. While enjoying the rewards coming from working with their own hands, they welcome technology as a fundamental part of the evolution of craft. Open source spinning machines, electronic weaving looms, and 3D printers, are just some of the technological instruments available today for makers to experiment with.

Happiness is usually linked to experiences able to evoke emotional connections. In order to create emotions in us, textiles and clothes need to tell stories recalling human skills and values. This book contains some delightful examples of such evocative tales. Just to mention a few: the hand-crafted garments made by *Phaedra Clothing*, *Carlie Ballard* and *Shisa Brand* show us the beauty of natural textiles applied to modern aesthetics. They all succeed in communicating stories reminding us of past generations, of the bond to nature and to the community. "A garment is a narrative, a piece that changes over time", Deva O'Neill of Phaedra Clothing.

To obtain sustainability, high performance and aesthetic all at once, it is essential to merge ideas and abilities from different fields. Whether natural or synthetic, the future textiles are likely to be the result of interdisciplinary collaborations between scientists, designers and engineers of any kind.

"Contemporary artisans are developing a brand-new connection to human skills"

LOVED CLOTHES LIVE LONGER

Growing up with a twin brother, who has always been taller than me, as a child I ended up wearing a lot of used boys' clothes. It was kind of frustrating, but I didn't usually complain, as my mother made it very clear: "These clothes are still good, what do you want me to do? Throw them away?" That would be inconceivable. So, you can imagine how grateful I was every time I received dresses and skirts from my older cousins! These feminine garments were the ones I wore until they fell apart and I would refuse to sort them out of my wardrobe for many years, even if I was too big to wear them! Later, during my adolescence, my family and family friends would participate in regular clothes swaps. I remember the joyful and special moments when I received a new bag full of second-hand clothes. I was thrilled, and would dig through the bag again and again with patience, picking what I liked and trying to imagine how I could customise them to make them fit. I would then spend hours cutting, patching, and fitting to make them my own. And I loved them for a long time.

I think this is why *Loved Clothes Last*, the title of the Fashion Revolution Fanzine #002 makes total sense to me. The magazine revolves around the emotional value of clothes in our society and how to keep them in use as long as possible. Indeed, if we think about it, our ancestors were able to make garments last several generations (and without YouTube tutorials!), but the vast majority of consumers today barely know how to use a needle and thread.

Since clothes became cheap disposable goods, the need of knowing how to mend them disappeared. Sewing machines are no longer a vital household device and people feel totally impotent in front of a small hole or a broken seam. It has become easier and faster to buy new garments than to learn how to properly take care of them. Learning repair skills means we can evolve into emancipated consumers. Furthermore, it is an act of disobedience against the wasteful and valueless consumption system dictating our way to relate to fashion. To say it in the words of the repair activist and writer Bridget Harvey:

"As repairers we are simultaneously unlearning while we learn. Rather than making something new, we intervene with that which already exists. These interventions potentially display our politics: they are slogans not shouted, but made. They show interdependences, and repair-making is an informative act in the midst of object lives, rather than a finalising design."

Disconnected from its aspect of economic necessity, repairing becomes a pure creativity mechanism showing us that we no longer need to be passive buyers. Through re-skilling practices, we grow into makers, innovators and creators of emotional value. *Katrina Rodabaugh* is a globally known writer and crafter, who brings together theory and practice on slow fashion. Her work illustrates the beauty of fixing and inspires a mindfulness and "mend-fullness" way of dealing with our wardrobes. The path to become more conscious consumers starts with looking into our closets to find pieces we actually have an emotional connection to and decide to love them as long as possible.

MAKING AMENDS

To buy cheap clothes, we all know, is not a good moral deal. It means to bring home garments carrying a story of sufferance and pollution. However, to buy more expensive clothes does not necessarily mean that these have been produced under better working conditions or with less hazardous chemicals. The high complexity of the textile supply chain and its global extension make it extremely hard to create transparency within it. So, how can we find the brands we want to be proud to wear?

Looking for fashion companies working within local supply chains or small designers producing locally is a great start. *Botanical Inks* is a modern natural dye business based in the UK. With their project "Bristol Cloth" they did not only recreate a traditional supply chain for tweed fabrics, but they also showed the immense power of the local maker community. Projects such as these are demonstrating the feasibility of modern sustainable local supply chains, sources of products we can culturally relate to.

Buying locally made products is key in re-establishing the psychological relationship between materials and their real costs, while finding a refreshed connection to cultural heritage. Weaving, printing, dyeing, and knitting are just some of the categories grouping a countless amount of traditional craft techniques all over the world. Many designers are rediscovering the significance of keeping these folkloric crafts alive and integrate them at the core of their business models. British weaver Imogen Di Sapia with her label *Bright Moon Weaving Studio*, blends and spins local wools to create her own yarns, which she hand-weaves into entirely one-off pieces. And through her woven jewellery collection for *Lesh*, Summer Moore reminds us that the beauty of crafts can be applied to modern forms and materials.

"Buying locally made products is key in re-establishing the psychological relationship between materials and their real costs"

Artisanal communities all over the world need to be empowered. Villages and communities that were used to life thanks to the commerce of their unique artefacts, are now squeezed by the globalised fashion industry. Their traditional techniques and skills are not of interest to the fast fashion system and these communities end up being exploited as cheap labour and their knowledge is lost. A wave of innovative businesses are fighting to change this situation. Brands such as *Calmo, Mehera Shaw, milo + nicki,* and *Carlie Ballard* working with traditional techniques in artisanal communities in Uruguay and India are fantastic examples of this new way of working with communities with the aim of preserving their cultural heritage.

"Artisanal communities all over the world need to be empowered"

In order for traditional crafts to survive the globalisation of cultures, they need the close collaboration of skilled people, factories and conscious designers. They need this collaborative team to create innovative ways of integrating crafts in scalable productions, to maintain their originality and integrity instead of misusing them. As consumers we also play an essential role. With our buying decisions, we have the power to celebrate diversity rather than uniformity as well as to support local artisans and their heritage.

We have the power to transform consumption into an act of mindfulness, slowing down the rhythm of the industry and reducing the volume of what we buy. The term "Slow Fashion" really refers to a different way of approaching fashion, where the artistic and artisanal aspects have higher relevance than the price or the trends.

The label *SHIO* in Berlin wonderfully demonstrates how fashion collection cadences can be slowed down to bring together craft, upcycling, and hand dyeing practices. The designer Kate Pinkstone, works with small quantities of certified materials to make only the number of garments needed by her clientele. The slow rhythm of her making allows Kate to experiment with natural dyes and upcycling techniques too.

Far from the possibility of a better future and deprived of their basic human rights and personal freedom, workers in the fashion industry often live in modern-slavery conditions. Today, compassionate entrepreneurs from all over the world are starting to set up strong businesses based on new values, including enabling workers personal and professional growth. One such business is the sustainable fashion brand *Mayamiko*, which provides education, sanitation and the transfer of working and economical skills to workers in Malawi. The empowerment goes even further, since the company offers micro-financing schemes for women who want to start their own businesses.

> "We have the power to transform consumption into an act of mindfulness, slowing down the rhythm of the industry and reducing the volume of what we buy"

Founded by the inspirational Paola Masperi, *Mayamiko* embraces sustainability as a holistic concept. But, within the fashion industry wages below the living wage limit are not just a problem of production countries. We can find exploited workers in most of the western world. London-based shoe label *Juta Shoes* is succeeding in creating awareness around this topic, as well as offering fair working wages to immigrant women. The two founders, Sabeha Miah and Joanna Hamer believe in the empowerment of local communities and in the teaching of crafts to raise the employability chances of workers.

Supporting local communities also means to include more disadvantaged people in our much too efficient society that tends to marginalise these individuals. The integration of workers with learning disabilities is at the core of the Spanish social enterprise, *Teixidors*. When translated to English, "Teixidors" means "weavers", conveying a clear message that their makers are the most important aspect of their business. Beside creating wonderful unique woven pieces, this company gives an opportunity to workers to carry out creative work in a totally integrative environment. The value generated by this business goes beyond the economic aspects: it is beneficial for the whole local community and its sense of belonging.

POSITIVE PROSPECTS

As you can see, the fashion industry is transforming itself into a colourful mix of innovative, inclusive business models that make profit without exploiting their workers or the environment. Modern sustainable fashion businesses understand their actions as a vital source of social profit, generating value for the whole community.

Woven & Worn is an inspiring collection of precious stories that together create a wonderful collective imagining of how the future of fashion could look, if we decide to shape it this way. As consumers we have the choice to jump on the train of this revolution and make our decisions matter.

BOTANICAL DYEING

Botanical dyeing in the form of bundle dyeing, also known as eco-printing, is a contemporary natural dye technique used to create unique repeat patterns on cloth, without the need for extraction or a dye pot.

This technique uses fresh, dried or frozen flowers and plant materials to create designs which capture the natural pigments and forms of the plant matter and have been described as psychedelic and ethereal.

- -

"I would rather have ten items of clothing in my wardrobe that are well made sustainably, biodegradable, and are going to last me the next ten years, maybe longer and I might even hand them down to the next generation"

Babs Behan, Botanical Inks

BOTANICAL INKS

Babs Behan
Bristol, UK | botanicalinks.com

- -

CREATIVE BEGINNINGS

I officially set up Botanical Inks in 2014, when I held my first workshop in the Barley Wood Walled Garden in Somerset, where I offered a natural dye block print and screen print workshop.

Previously, I studied Fine Art and specialised in drawing and painting, creating detailed drawings as well as abstract impressionist-style paintings. I have always been in love with colour, form, and organic shapes. I went on to study Surface Design at London College of Communication to find a way to turn my work into something more commercial. I learned to apply colour and print to different surfaces and it was through that process that I learned of the toxicity of the printing environment and materials used. I was shocked to discover how many chemicals were involved in the processes, as well as the plastic-based printing inks, and the waste that goes down the sink. Through a friend I found out about block printing with vegetable dye in Jaipur, India. I was completely lit up by it. I knew I had to go there and find out more; using all-natural materials made so much sense to me. I was very excited for the potential of non-toxic creativity!

In India, family-run businesses create stunning work, where every delicate print is unique. I visited Jaipur and studied with a master dyer. I learned how to transfer my drawings into block designs, which were carved by the master craftsmen. I then learned how to make inks and print – which I found very difficult, but was second-nature to my tutors. That marked the beginning of my natural dye journey.

"I was very excited for the potential of non-toxic creativity"

After graduating, I set up a clothing label and split my time creating and selling costume at festivals over the summer period, and in the winter months, I travelled around the world. For eight years, I recycled fabrics and used natural dyes and methods to create clothing. I went to India to set up and develop the business and started upcycling vintage saris and end-of-line printed material.

During my travels, I discovered a variety of natural dye traditions. In Peru I uncovered dyed alpaca yarn, whereas in Indonesia, dyeing was combined with wax resists to create stunning batik designs, and in Lao and Cambodia woven naturally dyed yarns were traditionally crafted. These varied experiences made me realise natural dyeing was happening everywhere, and that just because it wasn't happening in England, didn't mean it couldn't be a reliable method of production.

HISTORICAL ROOTS

The desire to investigate dye history led me to discover that England has a rich natural dye story and that it was only about a hundred years ago that we stopped using natural dyes in favour of synthesised chemical colourants. I find it fascinating and incredibly inspiring that England has such a deep natural dye history and I revel in the romance of the shipping routes and stories of trading. When the sea routes first opened, we started importing colours from all around the world and the trading routes transformed cultures and allowed them to blend and merge.

Suddenly England had access to a range of exciting colours and materials. We used these dyes for centuries, on a commercial scale – so I felt that there was no reason why they couldn't be brought back. Beautiful, vivid natural dyes have a natural allure, as they contain hundreds of colour pigments, whereas chemical dyes contain just one or two shades, so lack the same level of depth. Natural dyes are also reliable, and although there is some concern that they aren't as vivid and colourfast as synthetic dyes, it's simply not true. In fact, synthetic dyes are not completely colourfast, as they can fade in sunlight as well as through washing and wear. I believe we need to move away from the ideas of creating things that will last forever, and accept the ageing process.

At the time of the industrial revolution, coal was utilised for many different industries, and chemicals derived from coal tar were used to synthesise colourants. With a sudden influx of innovative machinery, and a market growth, production was scaled up to meet the demands of the emerging global mass market. In order to create the clothing, manufacturers required vast quantities of fibre and dye, and synthesised dyes began to replace their traditional natural counterparts.

In recent years, however, I have seen an explosion of interest in traditional and contemporary crafts. During my studies at university, art and design was shown in galleries and had more prestige, whereas craft didn't have a place, but now things are completely different. Craft is celebrated more as an art form. It's a much more exciting place than five to ten years ago. Of course you would appreciate the skill of a craftsperson who has worked to hone their skills and create a real thing of beauty.

AN ANCIENT ARTFORM
Naturally derived colours have been used in paint since the Neolithic period, around 10,000 BC. Ancient examples of natural dyeing of textiles were discovered inside Tutankhamun's tomb, perfectly preserved in time because they could not biodegrade. I'm very inspired by the history of this craft and the connection it gives us to another time.

INTEGRITY

My week consists of studio work, workshops, foraging, collecting wool or flowers, or general admin. Every day is different, and it keeps life interesting. To dye and eco-print natural textiles, I forage for local plants, windfall leaves and petals, as well as collecting herbs and seasonal flowers from my garden and recycling waste by-products, such as avocado skins and pits, and onion skins. In the UK there is a wide variety of species of plants that are ideal for dyeing. Common British plants such as nettle, madder, dock, and bracken provide an accessible supply of renewable dyestuff. Although we may not have a local source of bolder hues created by pigments such as cochineal, we have enough to provide the three primary colours and over-dye them to create different hues.

I exclusively use chemical-free, organically sourced natural fibres in my work. I source my natural fibres, including wool and silk from local British producers and I believe it is important to the integrity of the sustainability of the product that all the materials I use are biodegradable, non-toxic, and contain no harmful detergents or chemicals. To reduce my carbon footprint, it is also important to me that the materials I use are as close in locality as possible, and I prefer to supply the local community to avoid the shipping costs to the planet.

Working with local businesses, I have set up the "Bristol Cloth" project. I organically dye holistically farmed and biologically washed wool from a local farm and pass it on to the Bristol Weaving Mill, the first industrial loom to open in Bristol in almost a hundred years, to be woven into cloth. Bristol Cloth showcases British heritage and aims to prove that it is still commercially viable to make cloth that sustains British tradition, culture, community, land, and the economy.

Crafts demonstrate our heritage and our history and are something to be respected, preserved, admired, and shared with the world. I would rather have ten items of clothing in my wardrobe that are well made sustainably, biodegradable, and are going to last me the next ten years, maybe longer and I might even hand them down to the next generation.

I'd like to live in a world surrounded by handcrafted, organic, almost living objects that have their own personality. I believe we have a responsibility to understand the people and the processes we are investing in to make sure that what they are making is of benefit to the world.

EXPLORING THE CRAFT

To focus on learning the craft and understanding how to use all local materials, I participated in an art residency in the Cotswolds countryside. During my residency, I used foraged hedgerow plants, organic plants grown in the garden, local wool, and discovered plant-based mordants in an attempt to closely follow the soil-to-soil model of using what is around me, from the ground up, with the potential to be returned to the ground, as practised by the Fibershed organisation in California.

Another part of my residency was to teach craft workshops to local communities, and so I started to build the confidence to teach and share my knowledge. Positive feedback encouraged me to continue to offer natural dyeing workshops after my residency. I discovered that people are losing faith in the future, and are hungry for sustainability, so methods such as these give hope and empowerment.

At this time, I was living on a farm in Somerset, living off the land with thirteen other creatives. From there I started to build Botanical Inks. After moving to Bristol, I was approached to write a book on my creative practice and started getting very high-profile clients for workshops, such as the Saatchi Gallery and the Tate, and it just snowballed from there.

"... people are losing faith in the future, and are hungry for sustainability, so methods such as these give hope and empowerment"

MOTIVATION

Sustainability is reflected throughout every aspect of my life – I eat organic food and try to create as little waste as possible. It's a core value. One of my favourite printmakers is William Morris. He was inspired by nature and spent a lot of time in natural spaces gathering ideas for his work. When all other creative companies of his time were switching to synthetic chemical dyes, he was passionate about maintaining the use of all-natural dyes. He also built factories based on social principles, and considered the quality of life of his workers. Factories were built around courtyard gardens so that workers had regular access to green spaces. He wanted to be ecological in everything he did and saw the beauty in natural materials, appreciating the irregularities that made them so interesting. Like William Morris, I am very passionate about detoxifying the creative spheres wherever I can. I feel that we are currently living in a chemical era, and instead I want to invest in the natural world.

My work with Bristol Cloth demonstrates that modern sustainable textile production is possible and reliable and could be applied to many more aspects of industry. Through my work, I hope to encourage positive change that isn't coming from a place of fear and negativity. Spreading a positive message highlights what isn't working and increases awareness surrounding where products come from. I aim to inspire an interrogation of "fast fashion" and spending habits, and the production systems that they support. Working with the local textile community is also incredibly beneficial – there's power and energy in working in a group of like-minded people.

NATURAL CONNECTIONS

Working so closely with natural materials has enabled me to connect with nature and develop my eco-literacy. I have developed the ability to go out into a wild space and read the landscape in a completely different way. Foraging for plants to eat and use for medicinal purposes, as well as for crafting, feels meaningful and enriching. I am also more aware of the beneficial qualities of working with materials that are not damaging, and instead have healing qualities. I have developed an appreciation for plants and their many uses, as well as their aesthetic value. It's so exciting to be able to walk out of your door and know you can use something that is naturally there – it gives you an immediate connection and grounds you to the land that you are on. My craft supplies me with a completely wholesome experience – connection to nature, creativity and colour, and interaction with people; it allows me to engage with the world so much more.

"It's so exciting to be able to walk out of your door and know you can use something that is naturally there – it gives you an immediate connection and grounds you to the land that you are on"

WELL-BEING

Allowing time for being creative is very restorative and calming. When bundle dyeing, I try not to overthink the design and instead try to just be in the moment. The texture of the petals and silk, the aroma of the vinegar and flowers, the sight of the vivid colours – it is such a multi-sensory experience that I am able to escape from just being in my head and experience the process physically.

On a deeper level for me, since developing this practice, I have become more interested in plants and my relationship with them. Now, when I am working with plants I feel a more energetic connection and experience a form of meditation. I believe that learning to live harmoniously with the natural world and accepting that everything is interconnected gives you a respect for the world as a whole. I find spending time with nature helps you to feel aware of the rhythms and cycles of the world, as a living organism to be nurtured.

THE STUDIO

It's great to have a space that is set up just for natural dyeing, I have space for drying racks, pots and large heaters, with plenty of natural light and running water and electricity – it's so liberating! I can come to my studio any time of year, which is great because previously I spent a lot of time working from home or on the farm, in a freezing cold stone building. It's a great space but the next step is to find a larger space with room to accommodate larger groups for workshops.

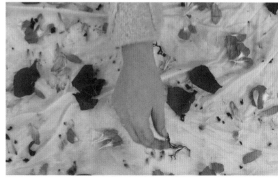

ECO-PRINTING PROCESS OVERVIEW

01 Before I start, I prepare the silk fabric for dyeing. First, I wash and scour the surface by heating it in a pot of water with ecological soap. Once cool, I tip away the dirty water and repeat the process until the water appears clean. For best results, I simmer the fabric in a fixative solution, known as a mordant, before dyeing.

02 I lay the silk out on a large workspace. (I work on top of another piece of cotton fabric so that I can capture the beautiful marks of the printing and dyeing processes). Using a mister bottle, I spray the fabric to saturate it with vinegar – I use organic apple cider vinegar because it is local to me. The acidic nature of the vinegar helps to brighten the colour.

03 To create an intricate speckled effect, I sometimes start by sprinkling the fabric with dye powder or extract powder. When activated with vinegar, the powders run together and blend with other pigments to create beautiful splatter patterns and a watercolour effect.

04 Next, I scatter a variety of plant materials across the fabric. Here I have used red roses, carnations, madder root, iron-soaked seaweed, and eucalyptus leaves. It is difficult to control the patterns created with the plant matter, so I tend to apply them randomly and embrace the spontaneity of the design.

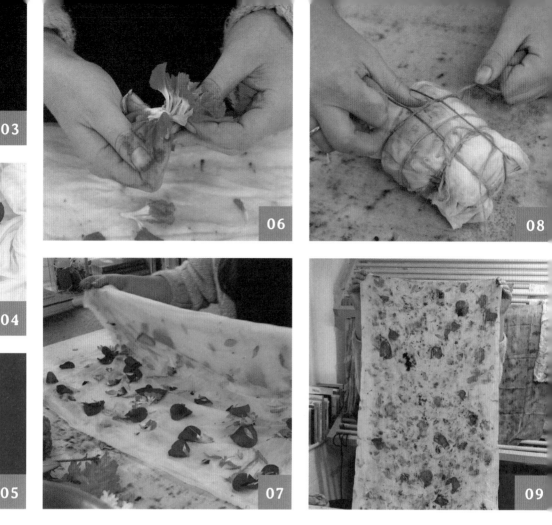

05 Once I am happy with the application of plant material, I spray the entire piece again with vinegar and fold the sheet in half across the width, sandwiching the loose organic matter between the layers of fabric. As the silk absorbs the vinegar, it becomes almost transparent, which is helpful when applying the next layer of plant material.

06 I apply another covering of vinegar to the entire piece and scatter additional plant matter onto the folded fabric. I tear the plant matter up and use single leaves and petals or leave them whole. To give the design space and the forms definition, I make sure to leave some white space.

07 I then gently fold the fabric again, this time down the length of the bundle. Once again, I spray the fabric with vinegar. At this stage you may see the beautiful reactions of the dye powders with the vinegar.

08 I continue the scattering and folding method until the bundle is as small as it will go. I tie the bundle together with brown string and steam for one hour, turning it over every fifteen minutes.

09 Once steamed, I unravel the bundle and reveal the floral patterns. I then hang the fabric out to allow it to dry naturally in the air.

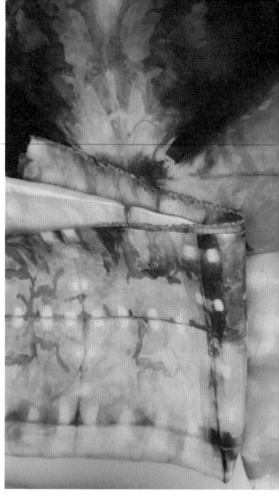

EVOLVING THE BUSINESS AND SHARING THE CRAFT

During the first few years of running Botanical Inks, my main source of income was from the workshops. I am now transitioning into creating more products. I consider my first product under Botanical Inks to be my book, *Botanical Inks: Plant-to-Print Dyes, Techniques and Projects*, which sells internationally. I now sell Bristol Cloth, which is available to purchase by the metre, and as finished products including bags, cushion covers, and tailored clothing. I also work on private commissions, creating botanically printed silk scarves, kimonos and keepsakes using bridal bouquets, as well as commissions for fashion houses and designers.

In the future I do see the collection expanding. Now that I am more connected with my local community and local tailors, there is much more opportunity for collaboration. I hope to work more on the Bristol Cloth project as it grows, however, I don't want to sustain the mass-market model. I'm not interested in the concept of scaling up in order to increase profits, because I don't see it as a sustainable approach. I see more value in keeping things small scale, with items that have higher value and are special. If I were to scale up my production, I would lose the all-important connections that make it so unique. Even with the Bristol Cloth work, which demonstrates a larger scale model, I would limit the amount that is made because I don't want it to be created for a mass market. I want other small producers to see a working model and be inspired to set up similar models across the world so that we have a collection of cottage industries everywhere, providing for their local bio-region. I don't see other producers as competition. I want to encourage others to copy our model and techniques because they are beneficial to the world.

THE FUTURE

I believe there is a desperate need for regenerative farming models that incorporate carbon sequestering and improve the quality of the air and soil. I have a firm belief that following closed-loop methods and considering our carbon footprint at every stage of manufacture has the potential to reverse the effects of climate change. In my opinion, it is possible for the fashion industry to cut out synthetic fibres and chemical dyes and processes and replace them with all-natural materials such as wool, whole fibres and plant-based dyes. Using the Fibershed soil-to-soil model to create fashion locally, on a global scale.

My dream future plan for Botanical Inks is to set up a semi-rural studio, run on clean, renewable energy, with a dye garden to grow organic plant-based dyes and mordants. With a reed bed filtration system, I would run a truly circular non-toxic factory and work as part of a local cottage industry, collaborating with local fibre growers, weavers, and tailors to create local biodegradable garments and accessories for our local community.

MILO + NICKI

Nicki Patel
Texas, USA | milonicki.com

- -

CREATIVE BEGINNINGS

We are milo + nicki, an energetic, indomitable duo who care deeply about those closest to us and the planet we live on. milo + nicki first began in 2008, the moment we signed the official adoption papers for Milo Patel. Fast forward and Milo and I are inseparable. We are attached at the hip – or is it tail? We have hit many highs and lows, and the ride so far has been a rollercoaster. Everything that happens to me seems to happen to him. In 2014, I hit rock bottom. With the paralyzing pressure to achieve and do more, combined with a few huge life hurdles, my health started to deteriorate. Being inseparable, my pup Milo's health began to decline too. And no doctor or specialist had a remedy.

I lived in fear of not knowing what the next day, hour, or minute held for us. I lost twenty pounds and two years, and still there was no diagnosis. In our pursuit to grow stronger and healthier, we turned to our roots. Family, love, and faith became our medicine. It is here I began to understand the delicate relationship between our bodies, the environment, and our health. Plus, I began to realise the impacts of societal pressures females face on a day-to-day basis as I was forced to choose between my career and health. I learned internal healing was just as important as external healing.

> "My designs are vibrant, always sustainable, and aim to empower women, and bring love, transparency, culture, and ethicality back to the world of fashion"

By combining my passion for sustainability, clean living, and a health-first mindset with a new understanding of fashion, and drive to bring awareness to a deep-rooted destructive consumer industry, I knew I wanted to create a brand that could be the embodiment for female empowerment – doing good, looking good, and feeling good. This is how milo+nicki was born. My designs are vibrant, always sustainable, and aim to empower women, and bring love, transparency, culture, and ethicality back to the world of fashion.

It's been a wild ride! But the love that we share with those closest to us, and the passion for the longevity of our health and our world, remain at the forefront of our lives. We will always be about the journey, and never the destination. As we conquer our fears, take a leap of faith, never give up on ourselves, and live a life of colour, we hope to empower others to do the same.

ENCAPSULATING SUSTAINABLE FASHION

milo + nicki is a cruelty-free, ethically designed womenswear line by women, for women. We are the first and only brand in the world to create an entire capsule collection made of banana waste. Everything we create is a true labour of love for culture, tradition, people, planet, and animals. Each piece is made of custom handwoven fabric that is hand tied by an all-woman team in India, hand dyed with plant-based indigo and madder root, and handmade in the USA. With one of a kind, timeless, and versatile pieces that are made to last for generations to come, I hope that these pieces become a part of the wearer's story as much as they are a part of ours.

> "I believe that women can do it all, so why can't the clothing we wear?"

The Bandhani capsule collection is inspired by my ties to and love for my culture, traditions, favourite festivities, and most of all, family. While keeping to a bohemian and free feel, the collection is also Indian and Zambian in spirit. The capsule collection consists of ten pieces that can be reversed, and mixed and matched to create over twenty-five looks, and ultimately, a suitcase full of all the pieces needed for a perfect vacation. The collection is biodegradable, sustainable, ethical, fair-trade, vegan, and cruelty-free. I believe that women can do it all, so why can't the clothing we wear?

MOTIVATION

I believe imperfection is perfection, and handmade is always one of a kind. The process for creating our pieces holds the same value, as each design is made with love and it can be seen and felt in every individual technique and garment. My favourite part of the entire process is seeing the story of each woman in our supply chain play out in the final piece; from our weavers, dyers, and seamstresses to our happy customers. It gives value to every piece of clothing that goes beyond dollars. I enjoy taking a concept I envisioned, sketching it repeatedly on paper, drafting up a technical pack to create samples, and finally seeing my pieces come to life through a model or a customer. But creating something unique, versatile, and designed for all women is what I enjoy most.

The preservation of culture and traditions is at the root of every design I create. I also believe in doing no harm to people, planet, or animals which is why I focus on making our entire supply chain as sustainable as possible. At milo + nicki, we weave our own fabric from the stalk and stem of banana trees, to give banana waste a new life and meaning. Our small team of women in India only weave, tie, and dye in small batches to ensure the process is ethical and sustainable, and we also ensure that we only use plant-based dyes to make certain there is zero toxic chemical run-off when our fabric is dyed. By producing small batches with a local family owned workshop, I am able to monitor production and make sure ethical labour laws and practices are being maintained. I hope to one day reduce our carbon footprint even more by moving our entire production to India to support the talented local artisans there.

Although the process is lengthy for a one-woman brand, it is something I wouldn't change for the world because it gives new purpose to creating a handmade garment that is sustainable, ethical, and cruelty-free. The experience of sharing our craft and design with the world has been quite difficult since many consumers don't yet grasp the concept of slow fashion, and how handmade our pieces are. I believe that there has been a shift in the overall fashion industry, but it will take time for people to rewire, and understand why things are created the way they are, and why they cost the prices they do. I believe there is a great movement for change.

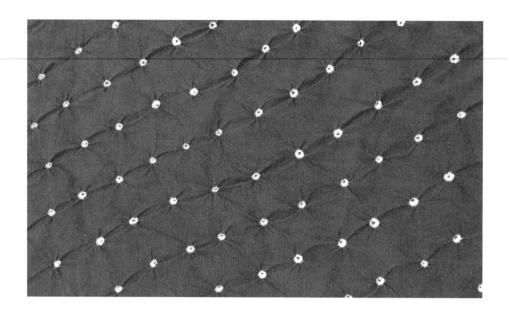

WORKSPACE

Being a solopreneur, I have come to learn to adapt and save space through primarily working in my own home for the vast majority of what milo + nicki entails. Occasionally, I will work from local coffee shops to get myself out of the house and network with others. I believe that being able to surround myself with the people I love, and my adorable pup, Milo, gives me the motivation and boost to keep pursuing what I love.

Our team in India works primarily from a remote village in Rajasthan, at the border of India and Pakistan. The village is very small so they have little access to modern technology which can make communication difficult between our western world and the eastern world they are used to. There is such beauty in their lifestyle that I love – living simply, closely, and connected with the things they love most, such as family and nature.

EMBRACE SUSTAINABLE MAKING

If you dream or aspire to create a sustainable or conscious brand, go for it! The best way to learn is to immerse yourself in the concept you wish to achieve, but also immerse yourself in education of the industry, the community (local, international, or artisan) you wish to impact, and remember nothing is perfect. Keep going and think of your end goal.

BANANA FABRIC AND BANDHANI
DYEING PROCESS OVERVIEW

01 Banana fibre, also known as musa fibre, is one of the world's strongest natural fibres. Made from the stem and stalk of the banana plant, the natural fibre is incredibly durable and biodegradable. Naturally water-resistant, banana fibre is also fire-resistant, tear-resistant, and recyclable. By using the stalk and stem of the banana plant to make the fibre, and in turn the fabric, we consume the entire plant and leave minimal waste. To begin the making process, we first harvest the bananas.

02 Once harvested, our all-female team of artisans in India work the banana material from plant to fibre. Through traditional hand processes the fibre is then transformed into a useable thread and intricately woven to create a wearable fabric. Each stage is completed by hand, with care and attention to detail.

03 Next, the artisans dye the woven fabric using the traditional bandhani technique. Bandhani is a tying and dyeing technique used to create different patterns in fabric. It is commonly confused with tie-dye and shibori, but has its own roots in India. The fabric is hand tied with thread to create tiny pockets of cloth. The term bandhani is derived from the Sanskrit verbal root "bandh", which means to bind or tie.

04 When all of the knots are tied across the entire piece of fabric, it is then dipped in all-natural plant-based dye baths made of indigo and madder root. Once the fabric has absorbed enough dye, the fabric is removed from the bath and left to dry naturally in the sun.

05 Once the fabric is dry, artisans rinse and squeeze out any excess dye and then leave the fabric to dry again. To build darker and richer colours, the fabric is dyed multiple times until the desired shade is achieved.

06 When completely dry, our team of artisans pull the fabric and threads gently to release the tied knots. The thread acts as a resist to the dye, and once removed, reveals a unique pattern of bright white dots.

07 Once our fabric is ready, it is shipped to New York City where our family-owned factory hand makes each of our pieces. Finally, the pieces are shipped to Texas where quality control takes place and orders are filled.

FORGING A PATH

It is my dream to one day be able to have milo + nicki be my sole job and source of income, but with any new business or brand there are many learning curves and bumps in the road. To make sure I am focused on my long-term goals, I do work multiple jobs besides the creative director, founder, and everything else milo + nicki. I am a freelance personal stylist for a company based in San Francisco. I also work as a freelance writer for local and international publications. Occasionally, I will model for local brands and businesses as well as teach English to children in Beijing, China as an ESL teacher. I believe that it is important to never lose sight of your end goal and always strive for more. Even though I am still learning, working, and growing every day, I think if you are passionate about something and put your all into the project, you will succeed.

> "I believe in a brighter future for sustainability in this world and I hope that building a community around the same ideas and visions will bring more light and understanding"

Being a start-up brand with a niche in sustainability, ethicality, and cruelty-free, I have limited myself to the reach and growth of other brands in the fashion industry, but my primary goal is to educate our consumers and bring awareness to our collections of one of a kind handmade garments.

Our collections are solely sold direct to consumers through our e-commerce shop which allows us to reach our international tribe. We occasionally collaborate with like-minded individuals who share our values and morals, and attend local events and markets to connect with people personally. The most important aspect of creating a brand and building a connection with individuals is keeping it personal and authentic – values I hold dear in my personal life. Through our social media outlets – primarily Instagram, our blog, and Pinterest – I continue to share our story, our mission, and values because I believe in a brighter future for sustainability in this world and I hope that building a community around the same ideas and visions will bring more light and understanding.

MODERN MORALS

When I first began to research sustainable and ethical brands in the fashion industry, I realised there was a gap in connecting minimalistic, sustainable design with modern and vibrant uniqueness that today's go-getting female is looking for. I wanted to fill that void by creating a brand that would embody vibrant, feminine design with purpose, intention and a story that could carry on for generations to come. My designs are contemporary as I tend to create a connection between trends I love and silhouettes I believe can be worn by various women and handed down for generations. There is a balance you can find in both worlds, and I am still trying to learn and grow every day by getting feedback and adapting to the needs of my own tribe.

Our designs are intended to be one of a kind, and preserve culture and traditions that are very labour intensive, and I do not have plans to adjust to keep up with fast fashion. I want the pieces I create to carry the same values and morals I hold true for myself. I am focused on creating investment pieces that will be valued, cared for, and shared. I believe that educating the consumer and connecting them personally to their clothing helps break the consumer barrier, and that sharing the story of the women from India to New York City helps create a personal connection between the consumer and our pieces. Finding value in your purchases makes them more impactful and important.

> "I want the pieces I create to carry the same values and morals
> I hold true for myself"

Having to move slowly to keep in line with slow fashion sometimes hinders my ability to use all my creative energy, but I make sure to keep using it in the way I share our story through our social channels or continuing to sketch new designs in my spare time. I believe modern technology such as social media is an amazing tool to connect to an international audience and allow small brands to reach individuals that they may not be able to reach otherwise. I always try to find balance in using social media, and spend time disconnecting from it because it can also hinder growth and creativity. I want to be able to share my authentic self, so finding a balance is crucial for me.

POWER OF THE PURCHASE

For those who want to use their purchasing power for change, a good resource is the *Good on You* app for clothing and accessories. Brand research and not being afraid to ask brands questions about their products and how they are made also gives you power as a consumer.

THE FUTURE

Although I love what I do, and learn more every day, it does get tiring at times. In the future, I hope to expand milo + nicki and create a small all-female team who can help support me in my day-to-day activities with marketing, content, design, and production management.

I would love to collaborate with inspirational brands such as Mara Hoffman and Spell. These inspirational women demonstrate the brand and business model I want to create, and are also great role models of balancing an international business alongside family and social lives. I really hope to be able to one day partner or collaborate with these amazing women.

In my opinion, the sustainable fashion movement is making great strides, but there remains a huge amount of work still to be done. I believe education is key, even if it is just starting with a small tribe. I truly believe that the power of education can do wonders for societal consumption, and even change the course of our world. I hope that more large brands join the sustainable fashion movement so that we can have a louder voice in creating change in such a destructive consumer industry. Global change is needed, and it is needed immediately.

UPCYCLING

Upcycling is the process of transforming waste or unwanted materials into new products of higher quality or of better environmental value. Scrap or disused textiles of all forms can be creatively reused to craft beautiful contemporary garments with the use of imaginative dressmaking and dyeing techniques.

While avoiding waste, upcycling also results in the creation of unique products with a one-of-a-kind aesthetic and value.

- -

"Buying less, buying second-hand and buying thoughtfully can go a long way"

Kate Pinkstone, SHIO

SHIO

Kate Pinkstone
Berlin, Germany | shiostore.com

CREATIVE BEGINNINGS

I established SHIO in February 2012 after moving to Berlin a year earlier. During that year I undertook an internship with a sustainable fashion label, and worked part-time in a vintage store while selling altered second-hand clothing and my own designs at markets on the weekends. I decided it was time to start my own venture, so I searched for a space where I could create my collections and sell them.

When I first opened my store, I sold mostly vintage clothing and upcycled pieces. I really enjoyed cutting up used and dated clothing to create more current and simplified pieces or just downsizing extra-large pieces to a more wearable fit. I then started to create my own collections under the SHIO label, using mostly linen and organic cotton.

I make two collections a year: spring/summer and autumn/winter. These pieces are modern essentials for every day, built from timeless silhouettes. I continue popular styles season after season to promote the idea of slow fashion and offer each piece in multiple colours. Both the upcycled and SHIO collections allow me to explore the topic of sustainability and work in fashion the way I want to – without the industry.

> "I continue popular styles season after season to promote the idea of slow fashion"

STUDY

My advice to someone who is considering setting up a sustainable clothing business is to study fashion design, sewing, and patternmaking thoroughly to understand all aspects of the production processes. This knowledge will save a lot of time, mistakes and money along the way.

MOTIVATION

When I finished my fashion design studies in Sydney, Australia I interned at a few large fashion labels. I quickly realised I didn't want to be a part of an industry that exploits cheap labour overseas. Ethically, it didn't feel good but on top of that there were always complications with production. Mistakes were made because of communication problems, and this led to a lot of waste. There was also a lack of connection with the craft. We'd send away patterns and samples and receive hundreds of pieces in return without really knowing who made them.

I really love doing all the sewing and patternmaking, and challenging myself to keep up with the demand. It feels good to be able to show and tell customers exactly where their clothes come from, and how they were constructed. They definitely appreciate transparency and the interest is growing. The SHIO store is a part of the *Green Fashion Tour*, a guide to green fashion stores in Berlin. It's great to be a part of a community of like-minded people and help in educating others about more ecological practices in the fashion industry.

> "It feels good to be able to show and tell customers exactly where their clothes come from"

I use mostly organic cotton and linen in my collections. Even when grown organically, cotton is a crop that requires vast quantities of water to be produced, so I'm exploring ways to use second-hand cotton instead. I love working with linen. Linen comes from the flax plant, which is resilient and can grow in poor soil, using far less water than cotton. Every part of the flax plant can be used to create a worthwhile product, so nothing is wasted. It's one of the oldest known fibres, but at the moment it only accounts for a tiny portion of the world's apparel fibre consumption. I'd like to help change this.

BUCKING THE TREND

I try to create high-quality pieces that aren't trend-based to try to combat the nature of throwaway clothing we've seen in the past. I never really know what is "on-trend" or not. I try to make clothes that appeal to a wide variety of people, are comfortable, and are well designed so people feel good in them. My pieces are built to be versatile and can be both dressed up and down when paired with different accessories. A lot of them are also designed to be layered with other pieces, so you can wear them all year round. It feels like consumers are growing tired of fast fashion and appreciate shopping with smaller brands – not only because of the difference in quality, but because they don't want to dress like everyone else.

I have considered outsourcing production to increase the quantities I can produce, but decided against it because I really enjoy this part of the production process and I believe I should stick to my strengths. I'm wary of handing this process over to others in case I end up with pieces I'm not happy with. I also want to ensure that wastage is kept to a minimum. I would rather hire a skilled person who can work alongside me in the studio where I can see every process of how my pieces are made. But I try to make affordable pieces so that they are accessible to a wide range of people, so hired help with production could also mean I need to adjust my prices.

> "I try to make clothes that appeal to a wide variety of people, are comfortable and are well designed so people feel good in them"

To compete with larger businesses, I aim to create a shopping atmosphere that is relaxed and personalised. I believe allowing customers the opportunity to talk one-on-one with the designer and maker sets the store apart. I can make pieces to order with a customer's specific measurements, no matter how big or small, and also offer a tailoring service so pieces fit the customer perfectly. This is really important to my business, especially for the upcycled pieces, as they are completely one of a kind. Offering this service can determine if the customer buys the piece or not and I don't charge extra for it as I'm just slightly altering an already altered piece. This deeply personal service is something that mass-production clothing can't offer.

The main threat to the sustainability of this career choice is trying to convince people to spend a bit of extra money and make a more sustainable choice with their clothing. In the end, fashion is a luxury, and it's hard to compete with the prices of fast fashion retailers.

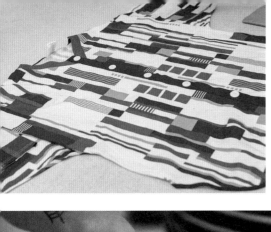

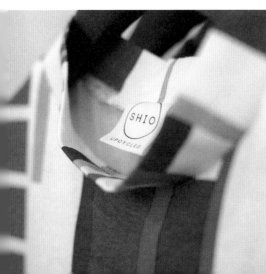

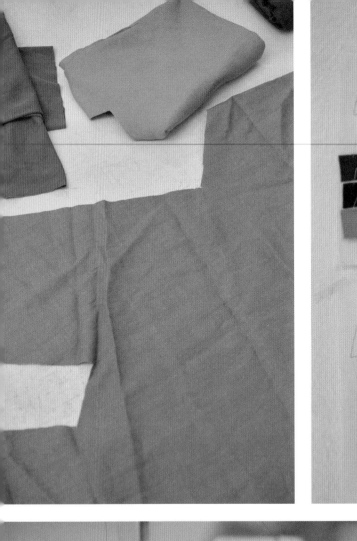

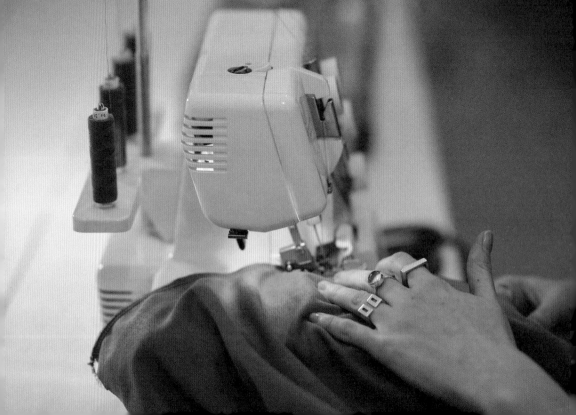

THE STUDIO

Having my studio connected to the shop allows me to work and sew during quiet times. Producing clothing on site allows me to keep track of stock and only produce what is necessary. It's nice to control everything from one space, as it allows me to experiment with styles and see which items are popular and selling, and which to discontinue. Interacting with customers is key to understanding what people want.

I'm lucky to have a big open studio with room enough for a cutting/patternmaking table. I create my own paper/cardboard patterns for the SHIO label. For this I need a ruler, tracing wheel, pencil, eraser, sharpener, and measuring tape. Sometimes I also use these patterns for upcycled pieces so the buyers can find the same designs made with a one of a kind upcycled fabric from a second-hand piece. This gives me the option to offer my designs in more interesting fabrics and prints than just the basic colours.

In my studio I have two sewing machines: an industrial Pfaff sewing machine and a domestic overlocker. I manage to make all the clothes with just these two machines. Working predominantly with linen and cotton keeps things pretty simple. I cut everything out individually. Before cutting, a lot of time is spent placing the patterns out thoughtfully in order to waste as little fabric at possible. I place weights down on the patterns and then begin cutting the fabric with fabric scissors. Recently I have been enjoying merging my two projects and including more upcycling in my collections. I use second-hand white cotton bed sheets as base fabric and print them with black tea and environmentally friendly black ink. This helps to hide any blemishes on the fabric and adds a touch of spontaneity to the collection.

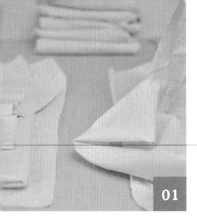

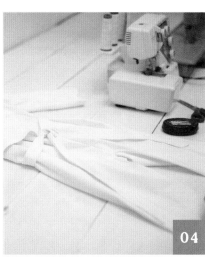

TEA-DYEING AND UPCYCLING
PROCESS OVERVIEW

01 I collect second-hand white or cream cotton bed sheets from local flea markets and thrift stores in Berlin.

02 I lay out the pattern pieces on the sheets, being cautious of conserving fabric and the grainline. If it's a plain-weave fabric then it doesn't matter if the patterns run parallel with either the horizontal or vertical grainline.

03 I use weights to keep the patterns in place, then cut out all the pieces.

04 Next I sew all the cut-out components together to create the base garment. Here I have made a jumpsuit.

05 I then make a tea dye using a tea concentrate which I made by brewing Darjeeling tea and simmering for two hours. I use a ratio of twenty teaspoons of loose-leaf tea per litre of water. I also stir in salt and fixative so the dye is colourfast.

06 I scrunch up a small section of the clothing and dip it in the dye. I then wring it out.

This creates a textured stain with the dye. I repeat until there are stains covering the entire piece, with enough room in-between to include black stains later.

07 I then let the tea stains dry. This technique works best when the fabric goes into the dye completely dry. If the black dye mixes with wet tea dye the colours will mix and you won't achieve the same strong textures and shapes.

08 I repeat the dip-dyeing process with environmentally friendly black ink. Dipping the fabric into the dye then letting it dry and heat setting it with the iron, means I don't wash any colour down the sink. Any leftover tea or ink can be kept and used again.

09 I have used this process to create a variety of different garments, including tops, dresses, jumpsuits, and trousers.

THE DAY-TO-DAY

I start my day with breakfast and a coffee while I answer emails and update the web shop. I then walk to the SHIO store, which is just two blocks from my apartment, and open up at 11.00 am. On quieter days earlier in the week I am mostly in my studio cutting and sewing and pause to greet customers when they enter the store. I usually like to start with restocking (making) the items that have sold in the store or online so I can make sure they're available as soon as possible. I'll then either work on patternmaking pieces for a future collection, sew pieces for a wholesale order, or work through a pile of second-hand clothing for upcycling – I enjoy this process the most. If it's a busy day in the store, more time is spent communicating with customers and doing general retail work.

My main source of income is through selling in the SHIO store; it's quite well established now after seven years. I also supply SHIO clothing to stores in Copenhagen and Lisbon. I run my web shop and sell on both Etsy and Trouva, an online marketplace for independent boutiques. I ship worldwide and use social media, especially Instagram to help with the marketing.

Social media has been very important for marketing and showcasing my work. Not only does it encourage people to come by and see the store and studio for themselves, it increases online sales, and has also helped people understand what I do. For example, sometimes people are unsure of what I mean when I say "upcycled". Some think it just means second-hand. But on social media I share a lot of before and after photos of my upcycled pieces so people can understand they've had a lot of work put into them.

I also collaborate with existing labels. Amy who runs the Australian label, Vege Threads is a good friend of mine and we enjoy designing a few pieces together and offering them through both our stores and web shops. This has helped in avoiding long-distance shipping as I encourage my customers from the southern hemisphere to buy from Vege Threads and vice versa.

THE FUTURE

As SHIO grows I would like to hire someone to work full time in the store so I can focus completely on the production. My weaknesses are sales and marketing, so I'd love someone skilled in these areas to help me with this. I'd also like to see the SHIO collection in more physical stores across Europe. Opening a second store in Berlin could also be an option if I find the right location.

I will definitely continue to explore methods of making clothes more sustainably. There's always work to be done. In my collections I try to avoid using many notions, such as zippers, plastic buttons, and fastenings, and when I do, they are always recycled. I do however, use polyester thread. I have tried using cotton thread but it's not as durable and constantly breaks while machine sewing, so it would also decrease the quality of the clothes if seams were likely to break open. I have considered using Lyocell thread, but at the moment I can only source it in white and it is not as cost effective for me. I hope in the future it will become more accessible.

I think there is a long way to go for the current fashion industry to become more sustainable but there are signs that change is on its way. I attend the Green Showroom and Ethical Fashion Show during Berlin Fashion Week and it has been amazing to watch this event grow and gather a bigger audience, attendees and participants every year. I think this is a good sign that the topic of sustainability is growing in the industry – in Berlin at least!

I'd like to see this interest go further and encourage more consumers to be curious, ask questions, and do their research before buying clothing. Buying less, buying second-hand, and buying thoughtfully can go a long way. The more people care about ethical practices, the bigger the difference we make, and not just in the fashion industry!

"In my collections I try to avoid using many notions, such as zippers, plastic buttons, and fastenings, and when I do, they are always recycled"

DEMANO

Marcela Manrique
Barcelona, Spain | demano.net

- -

CREATIVE BEGINNINGS

I established Demano in 1999 with two partners: my mother, Eleonora Parachini, and Liliana Andrade. The idea behind Demano came to us by chance. When arriving in Barcelona, we were astonished by the amount of advertising material the city produces every year. In Barcelona, large colourful PVC and canvas banners are used to promote exhibitions, events, and cultural festivals. The bright designs displayed across the city caught our eye and we considered how this waste material could be utilised.

One day, while walking down the street, we met some of the local workers who dismantle these promotional banners and soon discovered the banners' properties and potential as a textile material. On realising the strong, flexible, and waterproof nature of the material, we acquired a few banners. With the first banners, we made a couple of bags for ourselves and after receiving positive feedback from several people, we considered developing the project further. Demano was then built on the idea of transforming this discarded material into functional bags to be used on a daily basis.

We decided to share our upcycling idea with Barcelona's City Hall, as a proposal to give a second life to all the surplus promotional material produced in a year, which would otherwise be thrown away without any ecological awareness. We started researching the material and its production processes and conceived the proposal for the City Hall. We then established an agreement with the City Hall and with the cultural organisations producing banners to manage the waste promotional materials, and Demano was born!

We then established exclusivity agreements to attain the banners. It was an arduous job, but it was very important to consolidate an agreement with each organisation producing banners in order to reuse the material for our products. Before we could use the banners for commercial goods, we also needed to work with the original designers of the featured artwork in order to obtain the rights of the images and to make them part of our own design process.

Alongside securing permission to use the materials, we had to develop an effective and efficient production and design process. As the material comes from the urban environment, the selection and cleaning process had to be appropriate before it could be utilised. At this point we knew that we wanted the final bag designs to be an answer to urban needs, so our product range includes functional designs such as beach bags, bags for bike riding, and shopping. The concept behind Demano arose completely by chance, so taking the idea this far gives me immense pride.

MOTIVATION

Coming from Colombia, a country where nothing is thrown away and waste is kept to a minimum, I was simply amazed by the sheer quantity of waste advertising material Barcelona was producing year on year. I believe that all cities have huge quantities of wasted material which can be used in other ways. We work exclusively with waste materials in order to give them a second chance and another life, but we also enjoy using these materials because it gives us greater design opportunities and creative avenues to develop our original idea further.

Reuse and sustainability sparked our initial concept and is therefore at the very core of our business. When we started twenty years ago, there was not much talk of sustainability, it was a very new idea. Over the years however, I believe the interest in sustainability has grown exponentially and consumers are more educated about the type of products they buy. With their mere existence, our products create awareness of recycling and reusing, and it is one of the things we are most proud of. Besides being functional and aesthetically pleasing products, we hope that they also encourage the buyer to reflect on the things they consume.

At Demano we do not aim to make fashionable products. The idea behind every single piece we make, the concept that inspired us to create, is what we want to tell our customers. Our goal is to craft unique items with a history and an environmental awareness. We believe that working sustainably should not only lead to the design of the product, but also inform how that product is made. We are very proud to work with a network of small local workshops that would otherwise have disappeared because production would have been relocated. We believe that working locally is the best way to create community and pride, so we work with several social integration workshops, where people at risk of social exclusion learn to sew and are prepared to develop their own creative careers.

"We believe that working locally is the best way to create community and pride"

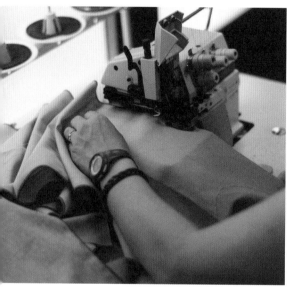

THE WORKSHOP

We have a space in an old industrial area, which over the years has changed and been reformed as a "cool" neighbourhood. We like it because many of our collaborators are nearby. It is a very bright and sunny space with an industrial style. Our team is made up of just four people: myself, my mother Eleonora who runs the shop, Mari Carmen Cascan who is in charge of the workshop, and Rosario Neira, our store clerk and photographer for online products.

When we started, we had never made bags from recycled banners before, so we had to develop the whole process. It is very manual work, which makes each product unique and different. Inside the workshop we use a hydraulic die cutting machine to cut the bag components out of the recycled materials. After the cutting machine, our key tools are our sewing machines. Although we have a method for making our bags, every time we work with a new material we have to rethink and adapt the way we work.

What we produce is dependent on the material we receive. We work with materials that come to us, so sometimes it is a surprise and each new material requires a different response and process. Besides the banners, we also upcycle other waste material, including old kites previously used for kite surfing – this material is used in one of our best-selling collections. We have also used textiles from the leftover fabric used to make umbrellas.

As well as our regular collections, we undertake collaborative projects. For example, we are currently working with a car parts company who want to recycle strips of paper-like material that comes out of their assembly machines. For that project we devised a method of weaving the material, using our own specially developed tools, and combined it with wood to create a collection of lampshades. To adapt our production methods, we partnered with a local CNC machine studio, who cut the plywood lampshade structure, providing a base for us to weave the recycled material into.

"We saw a need to recycle waste and took an opportunity to do something about it"

UPCYCLED BANNER BAG OVERVIEW

01 First, we receive the raw waste materials. This can include a variety of advertising materials and waste fabrics, such as banners, kites, posters and whatever we have been given to try out!

02 As these waste materials have often spent time outside, exposed to the urban environment, they require cleaning before they can be used. We clean each piece individually by hand.

03 Next, we assess the material and decide the best way to cut it in order to use the best of the design. We then position the cutting frames on the hydraulic die cutting machine and cut.

04 Once a batch of pieces have been cut out, we organise the components into piles for different bag designs. We try to utilise as much of the material as possible; using smaller pieces for wallets and coin purses.

05 To finish the product, the bag components are sewn together in our own workshop, with some designs being outsourced to external workshops.

DON'T BE FOOLED

My advice to consumers is not to be fooled by the term sustainability. Sometimes buying a product made near your home by a local person is much more sustainable than a product that claims to be sustainable and has travelled miles to reach your hands.

FAITHFUL DESIGN

Establish consistency and be faithful to your initial ideas. If you hope to develop unique and personal products, avoid the temptation to follow fashion trends.

WORKING TOGETHER

We sell our products in our shop in Barcelona, in our online shop and through national and international distributors, but we also develop special commissions for large companies. We work on specific projects to fulfil the particular needs each client has. For instance, we have worked for companies such as H&M, Coca Cola, San Francisco Contemporary Art Museum, and many more, recycling their advertising material and turning it into products that they can use as company gifts or marketing material.

It's great to see responsible practices from large companies in an attempt to work in a circular manner. Little by little, even at a very small scale for them, they are thinking about making gestures for the community and the planet, which is so important as they have the strength to communicate an effective message of awareness. It can be beneficial to both parties if big and small businesses can work together to improve for the future, rather than competing against each other.

"It's great to see responsible practices from large companies"

It is difficult to compete with the prices of mass-produced items, so we strive to make the most affordable product possible, but the craft and recycling processes can be more costly than the average industrial process. We believe that consumers have to be educated and understand the value of each product they buy – not only its monetary value, but its environmental and social value. We always aim to reach a fair price for everyone.

KEEPING UP

I spend most mornings in the workshop, organising production and developing new products, and some days of the week I deliver the materials to other workshops and see how the work is going. In the store I have an office where I receive clients and undertake administrative work such as social media promotion.

When we first started Demano there was no digital world as it is now and it has cost us to catch up. Now we endeavour to keep up with new technologies and ways of communicating. We believe it is important to show our customers the processes that we use so that they can understand how each of our products is made. We want to show that the banners and materials we use are real upcycled pieces and entirely unique. With the use of social networks, you can demonstrate what you can do to a global audience and it has quickly become fundamental in communicating our message.

THE FUTURE

To us, Demano is a very logical idea. We saw a need to recycle waste and took an opportunity to do something about it. I think the key to our success has been patience and dedication, as well as having a clear vision of the future. We have been very faithful to our initial idea and that has allowed us to continue existing. In the future we are interested in experimenting with innovative materials and processes. A few years ago we started working on how we could implement a zero-waste production. The idea behind zero waste is that we consider how we could utilise our own waste by designing new products or methods to recycle it. So far, we are reusing almost 90% of the material we receive.

I believe that being sustainable is not just about working in a few sustainable ways using recycling or waste materials; it is also important to be aware of the sustainability of the entire chain of production. Our work with local communities is fundamental to us and we understand the importance of teaching trades and helping to develop new jobs, for the future of that community, and will continue to do so.

WEAVING

Weaving is a process that uses two sets of thread to create fabric. Lateral threads, also known as the weft are interlaced at right angles with longitudinal threads, known as the warp, to form the basis of a fabric.

Fabric is usually woven on a loom, a tool that holds the warp threads in place while the weft threads are woven through them, in one of three basic weaves: plain weave, satin weave, or twill.

- -

"Weaving to me is not only a craft practice, it's a therapeutic practice"

Imogen Di Sapia, Bright Moon Weaving Studio

BRIGHT MOON WEAVING STUDIO

Imogen Di Sapia
Brighton, UK | brightmoonweaving.com

CREATIVE BEGINNINGS

I started Bright Moon Weaving Studio in 2016 as a way to reconnect with my textiles practice in a more therapeutic way. I'd just had my second baby and I was feeling a real urge to create with textiles again, and that meant adapting my creative practice to integrate motherhood somehow. The first year was mostly spent learning about weaving in my attic studio, working next to a sleeping baby, and exploring what it was about this craft that I found so soothing.

Through learning the craft of weaving, I could see a path into working experimentally with the raw elements of cloth-making; something that I had not really worked with during my previous training and freelance work in pattern cutting, couture, and costume design. By exploring the origins of wool and plant fibres, and studying natural textures and how subtle colours blend together, I found a way of communicating something of what I was feeling at the time. It felt like the right medium of making had found me.

I started weaving very large blanket-wraps to wear in the cold weather, long enough to wrap around myself and my baby when we went on walks; these also doubled-up as textiles for the home when not being worn. It felt important to make pieces that had a variety of uses, to reflect the versatile nature of textiles, and their inherent quality of providing warmth. I now make small-batch collections of blanket-wraps and larger blankets that use similar textures, the only difference is that I use a lighter-weight warp for the wraps, to make them less bulky and to give them drape.

I've always had an interest in wearable textiles, particularly historical techniques in pattern cutting and draping, and how best to interpret the unique structures within the cloth to reveal their secrets. I've taken that way of working and applied it to the way I weave; balancing rich textures in the weft and an openness in the warp which creates drape and depth in the finished works.

"I found a way of communicating something of what I was feeling ... the right medium of making had found me"

MOTIVATION

Weaving to me is not only a craft practice, it's a therapeutic practice which gives me time and space to reflect, and allows flow and rhythm into my life. Weaving in the way I do gives me a real sense of calm and happiness, as well as an opportunity to focus on making as a process, grounded in the physicality of the loom, and the textures of the yarns I work with. I really enjoy the process of watching a piece grow over time, and that I can't see the final design until it's finished and rolled off the loom.

Sustainability is an essential part of my craft practice, planned in to my weaving practice from the start, when I began working with ethical wool from a rescue flock. I had to decide if I would invest in this resource and adapt my working practice to the results of the initial research and development period. The ways I work sustainably are primarily on a closed-loop production cycle, which means that I do the majority of the work in my studio, working closely with two local flocks that provide me with ethical wool and alpaca fleece. The wool needs to be cleaned professionally so I send it to The Natural Fibre Company in Cornwall, which has a very high ecological and organic cleaning standard. The pros of working this way are huge; I know where the wool and fleece come from and that animal welfare is paramount, and I know the ecological considerations of cleaning are of the highest standard available.

Most significantly, working in this way means I have to work with the natural cycle of the year; from the initial shear to the cleaning and spinning; this all has an annual cycle that goes back for many thousands of years. I'm really proud to be part of that continuing heritage, and it also means there are historical precedents and techniques I can refer to and learn. As an immersive ancient craft, you can't help but be pulled into a slower rhythm of weaving. I'm very much inspired by the history of weaving, as it has such an ancient past and is fascinating to see what looms were made, how communities ordered wool work and weaving, and the songs, stories, and folklore that grew up around weaving as a skilled craft.

> "As an immersive ancient craft, you can't help but be pulled into a slower rhythm of weaving"

There has been a real increase in both the appreciation of craft and what it means for something to be handmade, the relationship to the past and what it means to go forward sustainably. From a professional point of view, I believe that craft awareness has grown; craft is being taken seriously as an art form and is now seen as an investment by collectors.

There is a very strong craft community in the UK and worldwide; I did most of my research online during long nights with my newborn son, and that's the beauty of social media – there will always be someone awake in the world to discuss projects with. I've also found the craft community incredibly generous with skill sharing via videos and workshops. An aspect I have truly come to value is that of collaboration with fellow makers, across many disciplines, not just textiles. This is a rich area to develop my own practice and try new directions in my work.

STUDIO SPACE

My workspace is really important to me, I've always had a studio space, whether in the home or in a rental space or desk share, and happily this year I've moved into my very own beautiful studio in central Brighton. It's lovely to be able to leave all my equipment in its rightful place and get to work straight away, it also helps the creative process because I can give myself time and space to consider work and take a slower view of design.

My key tools are my two looms; I have a narrow one for wearable wraps and a wider one for full-sized, heavier blankets. The looms I use follow the basic table loom design, called a rigid heddle loom; this suits my needs technically, as I work with very textured and variegated yarn, so I use plain weave, which only requires a single heddle.

The largest loom needed to be adapted and have a special bar made to take the heavier cloth, and also give me better tension. Ashford (who made my loom) were able to specially make me the adaptation and I fitted it myself.

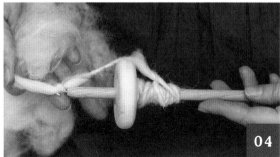

SPINNING AND WEAVING PROCESS OVERVIEW

01 To create a blended yarn, I prepare washed wool, alpaca, linen, and wild silk fibres. This informs the overall texture and colour of the finished design.

02 Next, I use English wool combs to prepare curly wool and align the fibres, while removing any vegetation. Textured locks can be added into the blend or separately during spinning.

03 When making a new blend, I start with samples on hand carders, adding in each fibre as needed. It's a good way of seeing how the fibres interact and which elements work best in terms of both texture and colour. I make a small "rolag" from this sample blend.

04 I then spin the rolag into a mini-skein on a wooden drop spindle; this is a nice way to experiment and assess the blend, and I can see if I have carded it enough to keep the fibres intact during spinning.

05 Once I'm happy with the sample blend and mini-skein, I choose larger quantities of fibre and add them to the drum carder to make a "batt" for spinning.

06 Next, I use a table-top electronic spinning wheel to spin the batts into yarn. The e-spinner is fast and easy to adjust to variegated textured yarn as I go. Once the bobbin is full, it goes onto a "Lazy Kate" stand for the next step.

07 At this stage of the making process I use a "Niddy-Noddy", a traditional wooden tool, to create skeins of yarn. I tie the end of the yarn from the bobbin around the centre of the Niddy-Noddy, and as the bobbin is on the Lazy Kate, I safely unwind the yarn into a skein, under tension. Once transferred, I tie the ends to secure the skein. It's important not to tangle the skein at this stage as it's full of twist and energy.

08 To set the twist of the skein, I soak the skein and then hang the wet yarn on a hook with a ceramic weight overnight. This method is used as I need as much of the elasticity to dissipate through the stretching process to make it a better weaving yarn.

09 The dried yarn is then put around a "swift", an adjustable stretcher which turns as the yarn is wound onto a weaving shuttle. I use a set of handmade wooden vintage stick shuttles.

10 To weave the yarn it is first added to the loom using a method called direct-warping, where I move the single heddle, up and down after each pass of the weft shuttle. Once the piece is woven, I cut the warp, knot the fringe, and cold soak into a "web"; to unify the warp and weft. The work is then dried flat and steam pressed to finish.

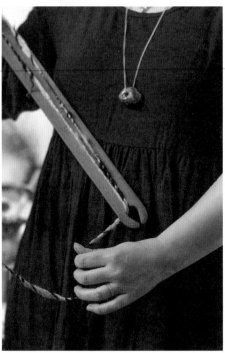

SLOW AND STEADY

I am a studio maker, which means I make small batches of work, designed by following the process of the materials I have to spin, and the yarns I've been blending; it's very much the opposite of "fast fashion". I mainly sell my work directly through my online shop, and through my UK stockist The Future Kept.

During my first selling season, I tested the water with a few different platforms to see what worked for me. I've tried contemporary craft fairs and traditional makers' markets and this year I will be focusing on selling through my online shop and collaborating with my stockists, and also by reaching out to an international audience who appreciate British crafts. I made a really big effort to launch my work in the UK as well as internationally, and it has been really successful. I have regular customers in the US, Australia, and across Europe. The best social media platform for my visual storytelling is Instagram, which I really enjoy curating. I also use Pinterest for collaborative work so each maker can add their images to the board.

I started my business from a place of making what I felt I needed to make, from an artistic place. Once I had found the right creative aesthetic, I was really open to seeing which pieces sold, what costs were involved, and what was the least stressful way of selling my work. There are considerations with investment and how you dedicate income and savings into your project at the right time and give yourself time; it's taken me two years to build a sustainable business to a place where it creates a viable income and is manageable for me with my parenting responsibilities. Craft-making is naturally adaptable to fitting around family life and I've had to learn mistakes from the past, for example, not taking on too much work when time is tight – handmade things take time, craft has built-in processes that need to be respected and that in itself gives me a pace to work at.

"... handmade things take time"

I have found that more people are now beginning to understand the reality of slow craft, whereas ten years ago the fast fashion system meant many people confused the instant gratification of getting the latest thing with the true cost and value of making things in real-time. There's been a huge leap forward in customers' understanding. There is now more awareness and appreciation that many makers need time to make their work in a stress free, creative, and contemplative way, and that that process could take a few weeks or months.

The beauty of this craft as a practice is that it attracts customers who align with, and support the sustainable and ethical practices I work with; there is no sense of competition with bigger brands, because customers want to know the story behind what they are investing in; they want to understand that it's handmade and has a philosophy and ethos behind it.

THE DAY OF A WEAVER

An average day starts with the school run, and then it's a short walk to my studio at 9.30 am, and time for a strong cup of tea. If I need to spin for a piece, I'll begin by choosing the fibres, and washing any that need it, then I'll use the English wool combs and drum carder to get the blend to the right texture and depth; I'll card enough for a 100g skein at a time.

After carding the fibre into batts, I then spin these into yarn on my e-spinner, which is a very small table top spinning wheel with a motor and foot-operated pedal like a sewing machine. After spinning the batts onto the bobbin, these are turned into skeins of yarn using a Niddy-Noddy. The skeins are tied and then soaked in cool water, then hung with ceramic weights for the night to set the twist and dry, ready for weaving.

After a mid-morning tea break, I'll get to weaving, because there is always something on the loom to work on. Then it's time for the afternoon school run and back home. I often do my online admin, blog posts, and social media updates in the evenings before bed.

INDEPENDENCE

Maintain an independent studio, where you are your own boss. There are ways of working with companies that can be financially supportive, but only if it works for your vision and won't compromise your core principles.

TRANSPARENCY

As my production process is completely closed-loop and transparent, I have a lot of pride in being able to tell customers how and why I work the way I do, and how that translates to investing in craft as a wider practice. Craft innovation in the modern world is a reflection on the heritage and historical practices of weavers and textile makers. This means I don't have to reinvent the wheel every six months, rather, my work can grow, adapt, and reflect the realities of the fibres I use, what's available seasonally, and how I approach my own practice.

Working smaller scale and truly sustainably doesn't present a problem in itself because craft makers are not mass-producers and there will be a natural level of making that creates income while supporting the creative process of the maker; it's the right balance, and I'm lucky to be working in that space. Any aspects of my process that I outsource are the ones I can't do myself for technical or time reasons, such as wool cleaning, botanical dyeing and sample spinning. Working with freelance spinners and dyers works well and the cost of all these processes are considered in the final price of my work so everyone is paid professional rates and treated fairly.

There is an existing way of working with textiles sustainably that should be the default and not the alternative. I think recent decades of consumerism and mass-production have given consumers a false perception of value, but I believe we are culturally becoming more environmentally aware, and better understand how supply chains lead to overproduction and waste; it's clear to see that the fashion industry as a whole has some very big questions to answer.

Craft is a community of living heritage that has always been there, and it has become culturally relevant again in the awareness of our collective impact on the planet. I believe sustainable design must be the way forward into the future. I don't think that beautiful craft should be considered a luxury. I think a shift in mindset would help here; if we all choose to invest our hard-earned funds into what we truly find beautiful, useful, and affordable for each individual, then we buy less but buy better quality and only what we need. I would encourage customers to ask questions and consider what's important to them; how does it feel buying something from a craftsperson, to understand their practice and all the stories that come with it? How does it feel to be part of a bigger cultural heritage of history and creativity?

> "Craft is a community of living heritage that has always been there, and it has become culturally relevant again in the awareness of our collective impact on the planet"

THE FUTURE

Part of being sustainable is considering the future of the work I make. A woven textile can last generations as an heirloom, equally it can be fully composted into the ground within a year. I'm happy that whatever journey my products go on, they will not have a negative impact on the planet. Developing a business like this really comes from a love of traditional skills and how they translate in this contemporary world of technology; sometimes simpler is better.

"Part of being sustainable is considering the future of the work I make"

My business goals for the future are simply to continue in the way this year has begun; gently, meaningfully and with a lot of happiness. I've decided that skills need to be passed on, so in the tradition of craft, I've taken on an apprentice and my hope is that I can share my techniques and offer training and insight into running a sustainable craft business.

I'm incredibly proud of my production model; it is at the core, sustainable, ethical, ecological, and flexible. I'd like to stay in this space and see what happens, these are very exciting times!

LESH

Summer Moore
New York, USA | leshloom.com

- -

CREATIVE BEGINNINGS

I was first inspired to start weaving after a trip to the Sacred Valley of Peru. I have a background in photography and was visiting the Amazon for a photo project, when I unexpectedly became fascinated by the woven textiles I'd see in the villages of Urumbumba and Pisac in the Andes mountains. I was especially inspired by the beautiful antique pieces – one in particular was almost unravelling, which allowed me to visually dissect how it was made. I was in complete awe of it, trying to figure the process out. When I returned to New York I enrolled in a weaving class where I learned how to use a loom to create basic patterns.

> "I'm drawn to the systems, patterns, and mathematics of weaving, and revel in the endless possibilities"

I had the idea to craft jewellery pieces early on in my practice, and would go in during studio hours and experiment with weaving on my own. I had so many ideas, patterns, and palettes I wanted to try, and the smaller scale allowed me to sample these ideas. I enjoy the repetitive aspect of weaving patterns, but I also thrive on variation within that repetition. I'm drawn to the systems, patterns, and mathematics of weaving, and revel in the endless possibilities.

I really get into the zone and work instinctively while weaving, so it was very interesting to learn that my grandmother, who was a big creative influence on me as a child, had also been a weaver. I wish we could have had a chance to work together, but I still feel weaving in my heritage, which is why my brand is named after my grandmother's maiden name: Lesh.

MOTIVATION

I'm very inspired by the vast history of weaving, especially geographically. It has been an incredible experience to travel and see what distinct aspects each culture has brought to textiles, as many of these techniques have been passed down through generations. I especially feel a kinship with the Bauhaus weavers. The fibre work created by Gunta Stölzl and Anni Albers during those years was ground-breaking and I have a deep appreciation for their experimental use of warp and weft to create modern geometric patterns.

Creating new woven patterns and colour palettes is where I find the most joy. Imagining an initial design and making it a reality through handwork is such a rewarding process. When digital photography became prevalent and I could no longer afford to print film, weaving filled the making void. Through this experience I've learned that working with my hands is key to my happiness.

> "Imagining a design and creating it through handwork is such a rewarding process"

Considering sustainability is crucially important to me because I understand that natural resources are not everlasting. It's important to use only what we need, reuse what we can, and be mindful of where our goods and materials come from. When I first started sourcing materials for weaving, it was essential to me that they were natural fibres, and that they were produced in an eco-minded way. So, I did some research and was able to find that my favourite cotton fibres were produced in Brazil, and the company was on the same page with their environmental and ethical practices.

> "... when making a product, there is always give and take in being sustainable"

For the more finely woven work in my pieces I use a strong synthetic thread to prevent snapping from tension. At first, I was apprehensive about incorporating synthetic fibres into my work, but when I researched the thread, I learned they were made from 100% recycled plastic bottles. I was so excited to see that this was even possible, and it has turned out to be one of my favourite materials to use.

The positive to being mindful of sustainability when working is that you're helping to reduce waste and toxicity. A big challenge is that it's difficult to be completely eco-friendly when making a product, there is always give and take in being sustainable.

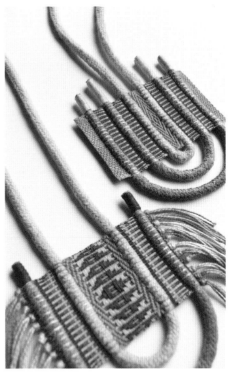
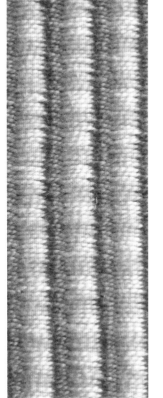

STUDIO SPACE

My current workspace is a dedicated studio within my home. I had a separate studio space for a few years and loved being a part of that creative community in Brooklyn, but it is also amazing to get work done any time of day (even in your pyjamas) without leaving the house.

The most important tool I use is my loom, which is a small four harness table loom that is perfect for the scale of my pieces. A warping board and lease sticks are also essential, and help to keep fibres taut and in order. Warping the loom is the foundation to any woven piece, and the end product largely depends on this first step. I tend to not use shuttles while weaving, unless I'm making larger swatch samples. A good pair of pointy scissors are always helpful as well.

I have made some small adaptations to better suit my weaving needs. I started using sushi rollers instead of kraft paper to roll the warp onto the beam, which helps create a more even tensioned warp.

WOVEN BRACELET PROCESS OVERVIEW

01 First, I need to choose a colour palette. This is the fun part, I love to mix neutrals with more vibrant colours, or create palettes that are inspired by art I've seen.

02 Next, I decide on which pattern to use. I will either come up with a new pattern, or create a variation of a design I've used in the past.

03 To start the weaving process, I first need to create the warp, using a warping board. I tautly wind the yarn around the pegs on the board. This determines how wide the pieces I'm weaving will be and keeps the yarn in order.

04 This is one of the more complicated steps in the weaving process, which involves rolling the warp yarn onto the beam and using a reed hook to thread each line of yarn one by one through the heddles. The harness order in which they're threaded determines the patterns that are possible. For the final step of warping the loom I thread the yarn through the reed.

05 I then weave the weft yarn through the warp yarn. For the *Petit Bracelets* the weft is made only of thread, but I mix in various fibres when making necklaces. The chosen pattern will determine which lever of the loom I press and which colours I use.

06 To complete the bracelet, I twist and knot the yarn to create the bracelet strap.

> "I really get into the zone and work instinctively while weaving, so it was very interesting to learn that my grandmother, who was a big creative influence on me as a child, had also been a weaver"

01

02

03

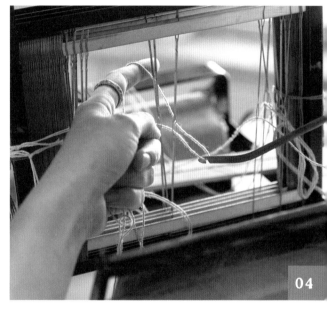

04

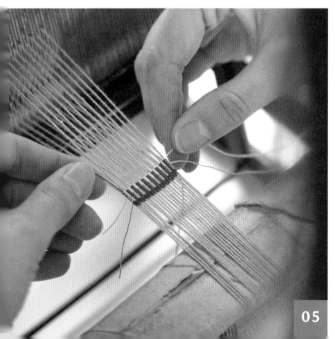

05

06

THE DAY-TO-DAY

A key source of income for me is through my freelance work as a prop stylist on photoshoots. This allows me to have two creative outlets and make my own schedule. I sell my pieces through my website, boutiques, and also attend markets and design shows from time to time. I sell both in the US and abroad. I have wholesale accounts with smaller boutiques as well as museum shops and I have also been asked to fulfil orders for large corporate stores, but I prefer to work with smaller boutiques as the scale is more manageable. There are many large retailers whose ethical and environmental practices are questionable, and I have turned down fulfilling orders for this reason.

"... weaving brings a calmness to my life"

Depending on whether I have web shop orders, design shows, or markets, my day consists of either warping the loom or using the warp I've already set up to hand weave necklaces and bracelets to fulfil what's needed. I start by weaving variations of patterns I have used on prior pieces, or come up with brand new ones. I work very intuitively and try not to overthink it, often the patterns come to me as I work, other times they're predetermined.

Finding the time to experiment and work on new ideas can feel constrained at times, especially while growing another freelance career, but weaving brings a calmness to my life. It's the moment and space I give myself to focus on experimenting creatively. I often feel a relief after weaving a piece, there's something about focusing intently on the pattern and process that's very therapeutic.

BE EXPERIMENTAL

You have to really love what you're creating and believe in it. Be experimental in your process, and try to create something authentically your own, rather than what's on trend. If you're just starting out, I would ease into turning it into a full-time business and stopping other sources of income. And be patient, there are very few overnight successes.

A CRAFTING RENAISSANCE

I have noticed more people embracing handmade goods, as well as learning how to make their own pieces. I started weaving just before the maker movement took full swing, so it was pretty serendipitous to be active during this crafting renaissance. There is a nice sense of community among weavers and fibre artists as a whole; it's amazing to see so many creative interpretations of a practice that has been happening for thousands of years.

Inspired by traditional weavings, I prefer to create pieces with longevity and don't adhere to trends. I think fast fashion is sadly creating more waste than we know how to process in order to keep trends cycling through and to coerce people to buy. I prefer to have and create fewer, well-made items that will last through construction and style. I'm not interested in outsourcing my making process in order to make larger quantities of jewellery, but I would like to offer more affordable smaller pieces for those who love the Lesh style, but may not be able to acquire the larger pieces. In the future I may consider collaboration and outsourcing if it can be done in a fair and community focused way.

> "It's amazing to see so many creative interpretations of a practice that has been happening for thousands of years"

One of the biggest threats to small creative businesses is having larger corporate companies replicate and reproduce their work without permission or compensation. For many makers, creating unique and distinctive pieces is part of their livelihood, and when that work is copied by larger companies it takes away from the handmade character, and puts money into the wrong hands.

BUY WHAT YOU LOVE

Buy fewer, better quality items that you will wear often, shop at thrift stores, and donate your own goods. Only buy what you love, not what's momentarily trendy. And remember to look into where and how items are made.

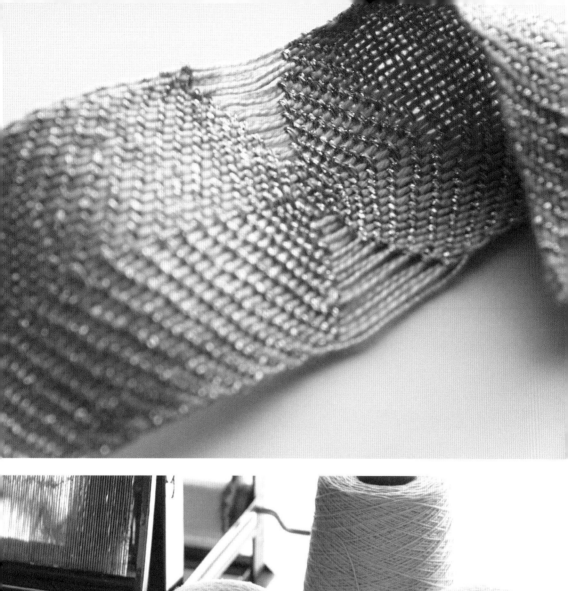

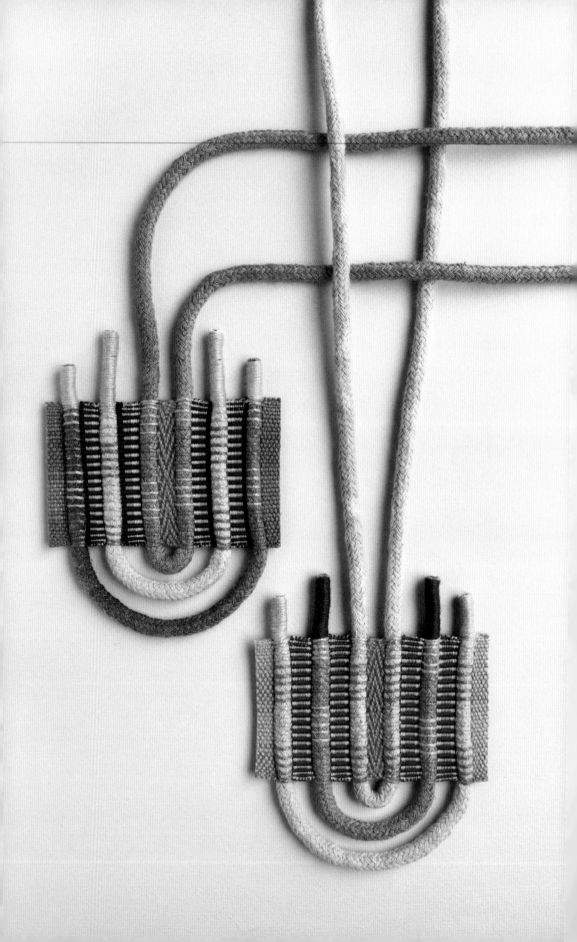

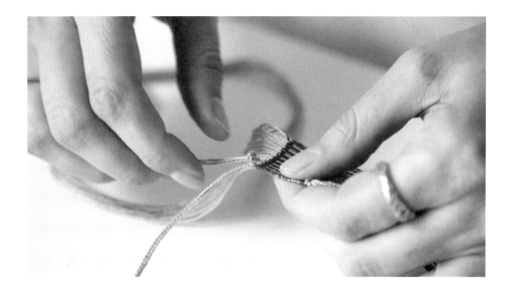

THE FUTURE

I recently started to incorporate ceramics into my woven collections and I am also in the process of making woven swatches for fabrics that I hope to have produced to provide the basis of a home goods line in the future. I enjoy experimenting and layering mediums to see what new ideas emerge. I think of Lesh as something broader than handwoven jewellery, and try not to restrict myself. When it's time to explore new ways of working I am naturally drawn to new processes. I will always want to create with my hands, and I think sustainability will always be a factor in whichever medium I choose. It can be as simple as recycling and conserving materials, or choosing to source materials in the most eco-friendly way possible.

I hope to see a decline in fast fashion. The fashion industry has doubled their production of clothing since 2000, which has far surpassed our population growth. This has led to billions of pounds of textile waste entering our landfill, or even being burned, causing toxic fumes to enter the atmosphere. The quick rotation of disposable trends has aided in this problem. I hope to see more companies turn to natural and recycled materials, and that these items become more universally affordable. I would also like to see more transparency in how and where products are made.

GET CREATIVE WITH MATERIALS

I would suggest doing research when choosing which materials to craft with, and getting creative. Find supplies around the house to use instead of purchasing or creating more waste.

TEIXIDORS

Barcelona, Spain | teixidors.com

- -

CREATIVE BEGINNINGS

Teixidors is a social project whose main objective is the social and occupational integration of people with learning difficulties through textile crafts. The project began in 1983 in an old factory located in a town closely linked to the history of the Spanish textile industry, in Terrassa, Barcelona. Marta Ribas, a social worker specialising in mental health, and her husband Juan founded Teixidors in order to provide a steady and stimulating occupation for those with mental health disabilities. An occupation where a person with a disability gets the chance to demonstrate their tremendous making abilities. The Teixidors project is based on the creative and pedagogical singularity of the interaction between the weaver and the loom; to constantly focus, count, coordinate, and measure.

The manual loom is the essence of Teixidors: where a disabled person can become an expert with an incredible capability to transform raw materials into exquisite shawls, to be sold in some of the world's most exclusive stores. The art of weaving requires constant interaction by the weaver; to focus and count the passes of the shuttle. The weaver has to coordinate the movement of two, four, sometimes even six different treadles and measure the pressure of the beater on the warp and weft – skills that take years to perfect.

> "It is a process of creation full of subtleties in which each weaver leaves a stamp of individuality"

It's the precise movement and meticulous skill of the weaver that transforms raw materials into beautiful handwoven pieces. The loom moves with the energy of its operator in a interchange of rhythms, in which the loom translates the weaver's movements into a permanent crossing of threads. It is a process of creation, full of subtleties, in which each weaver leaves a stamp of individuality. Every piece we make is unique and woven in the highest quality natural materials, including European linen, cashmere, Merino wool, and yak wool from Mongolia. We produce scarves, shawls, and ponchos, as well as blankets, throws, and cushions. Our pieces are stocked by shops that want to differentiate themselves and reach a discerning consumer segment. These shops have a genuine interest in a product that has a high design value, use high-quality natural materials and that is sustainably produced in Europe – the opposite of fast fashion. We are witnessing a change in buying habits and see a market that wants to step away from rapid consumption and focus on individuality. The social aspect of the Teixidors brand is becoming more and more interesting to the consumer. People want to support a "good" project if they are given the choice.

MOTIVATION

Teixidors is first and foremost about assuring a steady workflow for our weavers, to help prevent social exclusion through creative labour opportunities. The manual loom is a versatile, complex, and continuously demanding tool that acts as a stimulus for concentration, coordination, and learning. Learning to weave at this level is a slow process but with an exceptional result in the training of expert craftsmen. Adding a high level of design has been key to elevate the brand to a level where you can better understand the value of the product. Not only is it a handmade product, created in a natural material of very high quality, it is also accompanied by a design and production method that gives it its own identity.

The integration of people at risk of social exclusion and the commitment to responsible consumption form part of the sustainability of Teixidors. We believe in sustainability as a global environmental and social concept – it's been a crucial component of Teixidors from the very beginning. Every product in our catalogue is woven, washed, and finished in our workshop. While it's much too common throughout the textile industry to use cheap materials and add chemicals in the production process to manipulate the material into becoming softer, fluffier, and more malleable, at Teixidors we simply try to bring out the best in natural materials through the use of ecological soap.

> "We believe in sustainability as a global environmental and social concept"

The way we have chosen to source the majority of our materials also preserves sustainability as a priority: our Merino wool comes from a small farm in the Provence region of France. We work with one farmer and buy his entire production of wool each year. This wool is washed and combed at a GOTS certified facility and we make most of our own yarn right here in Terrassa.

For many years we have purchased yak wool and cashmere from two cooperatives in Mongolia that were started by Veterinarians Without Borders in order to secure fair salaries and responsible production in this region. We are constantly on the lookout for new and interesting materials that are sustainably produced – we think it's our responsibility to make this a priority whenever possible. This enables us to enrich the product from the very essence of the fibre.

The Ar Arvidjin Delgerekh cooperative, run by nomadic herdsmen in the Kanghaï mountains of central Mongolia, supplies our yak wool. This initiative is led with the goal of preserving the unique, fragile ecosystem that is the yak's habitat, in harmony with nature. The herdsmen include yaks in the region's indigenous herds in order to sustainably manage the grasslands and control desertification. This unique natural fibre helps preserve the country's rich nomadic tradition, while enabling the members of the cooperative to manage their future.

INTRINSIC VALUE

As we use manual looms, we can give our pieces a deliciously imperfect finish, often highlighted by a coloured thread that has now become one of our distinguishing features. Artisanal woven pieces are not uniform; they are full of nuances that reflect the characteristics of the tool used to create them, and the individuality of each weaver.

We focus on producing a product with a timeless design, of the highest quality with the unique value that craftsmanship offers. It is a product with dignity and a fair quality/price ratio, which means it is neither cheap nor expensive. Simply, we focus on appealing to an audience that appreciates the design and quality, and is sensitive to sustainable projects that consider the environment and the people employed.

It has been widely documented that global handicrafts are growing, especially as the market is shifting from what are considered ethnic designs to more contemporary patterns. We see a growth in requests from luxury hotels and designers who want to provide something very special and know that handwoven pieces offer this exclusivity. The rise in travel and tourism is also helping drive the demand for handicraft and the desire for pieces with meaning and gifts that cannot be easily found in other markets.

> "Artisanal woven pieces are not uniform; they are full of nuances that reflect the characteristics of the tool used to create them, and the individuality of each weaver"

Through its products, Teixidors aims to transmit a system of values in which the most important is the human factor: from the producer of raw materials and artisans, to our clients and consumers. Together we make the viability and the future of the project possible. There is no automation in the processes used at Teixidors: people enrich the product at every stage, taking advantage of the versatility of our looms and the artisanal character of our entire process. The manual elaboration of artisanal products is not based on efficiency but on singularity and this is where Teixidors seeks to add value in all facets of production in order to differentiate its value in the market.

We are committed to the use of natural fibres that are also renewable, local and totally traceable. Our products don't require sophisticated finishing processes. Because we use high-quality natural materials, we simply have to find the appropriate combination of eco-friendly soap, temperature, and washing time to bring about the transformation that will reveal the natural and intrinsic qualities of each piece.

THE WORKSHOP

At Teixidors, we have nineteen looms and each one was built in our workshop. It's a type of loom that has existed in Europe since the beginning of the industrial revolution. The design has been slightly adapted to meet our needs.

Teixidors has recently moved to a former textile factory. This new space will provide us with the opportunity to accept the many requests we get from schools and companies to visit our unique workspace and to show and educate this audience on the value of incorporating sustainability and traceability practices throughout the production process.

COMMUNITY AMONG CRAFTERS

Try to support other craftsmen whenever possible. For example, every year we weave beautiful blankets for two craft projects in France. These projects promote the beautiful wool that is harvested every year in their specific region by turning it into special traditional pieces that speak of the history of the region. We can put a warp of twenty or thirty into production, something that may not be possible in a bigger production facility.

WOVEN SCARF PROCESS OVERVIEW

01 First, artisans lace the threads that form the base of the fabric in the warp orientation of the loom. They pass the thread through the loom meshes and comb to ensure they correspond with the chosen pattern. The bobbin containing the weft thread is then added to a shuttle to cross the warp threads.

02 Using their hands and feet, the artisans work different mechanisms of the loom to weave the threads of the warp and the weft together and to create the fabric.

03 As the fabric is being created, the measurements of the piece are checked closely to ensure the pattern is followed accurately and mistakes are not made.

04 Once the piece is woven and before it is washed, the measurements and the quality of the piece are checked thoroughly. Artisans make alterations to the piece if necessary.

05 After inspection, the woven fabric is washed with water and ecological soap. Through the washing process the fabric is transformed and acquires the final soft touch and volume. The fabric is then passed through an iron.

06 To finish, all products are labelled by hand and individually packed, ready for the consumer to cherish and enjoy.

"There is no automation in the processes used at Teixidors: people enrich the product at every stage, taking advantage of the versatility of our looms and the artisanal character of our entire process"

01

02

03

04

05

TEIXIDORS

06

GLOBAL REACH

Teixidors handwoven blankets and scarves can be found in select stores around the globe. Currently, the brand is present in the main Spanish cities and internationally in Germany, Italy, France, Austria, Sweden, the United Kingdom, Japan, and the USA. Today we see most of our growth outside of Spain. Export now accounts for 60% of our sales. We also participate in several international trade and design fairs and depend on them to meet with our existing clients and to try to reach new customers. In countries such as USA, a product made in Europe is highly valued and even "made in Barcelona" is an added benefit. We are also seeing some growth in the Chinese market where a product woven on a manual loom is considered a unique product, impossible to replicate.

Social media is very important to reach a broader audience, to voice our values, and communicate our philosophy in words and imagery. We are present on most social media channels, such as Facebook, Instagram, Pinterest, LinkedIn, and YouTube. We also try to be very responsive to any requests from the press to receive images or to provide information about our products, processes and project.

A growing market for us is boutique hotels that are looking to create a unique experience for a demanding client and therefore want to source bespoke textiles for rooms and public areas. This has proven to be a fantastic window display for potential new clients from all over the world.

CONSTRAINTS OR STRENGTHS?

Over the thirty-five years since it began, Teixidors has been able to cope with the ever-changing circumstances of a difficult sector. Conspicuous consumption has reached an unsustainable point and at Teixidors we want to be at the forefront of this movement away from throwaway attitudes. We don't have unlimited capacity for growth, but we believe this is our strength. In many ways our constraints are in fact our strengths. Our limitation of increasing production is a strength for buyers who desire a unique product. The time it takes to train new weavers plays into the same strength, or constraint. Even the meticulous way we have decided to source our materials is a restriction that can be seen as force for good.

> "We are conscious of preserving the commitment to handwoven, while keeping the right balance between efficiency and economic sustainability"

We believe that it is very important to share with consumers that Teixidors products are made through a social project. While in the past sharing the message of the social aspect of the company may have generated some doubt about the quality of the products or the level of design, we now feel that not sharing this message means the consumers are unaware of their role in a very important project for a better society. We have seen that there is clearly a market audience that, when given a choice between two products with high levels of design and quality, is committed to a product that offers this added societal value. We are conscious of preserving the commitment to handwoven, while keeping the right balance between efficiency and economic sustainability.

> "We believe it's crucial to find your own specific market niche"

The soul of Teixidors is its weavers and manual looms – there is no compromise on this strategy. We would only consider outsourcing if it meant a collaboration with another socially conscious workshop. We also believe that competition is healthy and can only make us better. By studying what successful sustainable brands do well, we can refine our strategy, but never waver from our core values and always set our own path. We believe it's crucial to find your own specific market niche.

MARKET EVOLUTION
Consider the importance of incorporating design and innovation to develop products for the current demands of the market. And be aware of how the market and its needs evolve and change over time.

THE FUTURE

We have launched a collaboration with renowned British designer, Faye Toogood. All of her pieces are handmade by small-scale fabricators and traditional artisans, so she was especially thrilled about the handwoven artisan aspect of our production and the fine natural materials. The result of this collaboration is three beautiful handwoven blankets which were presented at the international design fair Maison & Objet, Paris and at the International Contemporary Furniture Fair, New York. In the future, we would like to explore more of these possibilities to develop collections and special products together with new designers, to combine the values of creativity and handmade processes in a social project. The collaborative process brings us new ideas and challenges, and product developments can progress easily and smoothly with the use of our large workshop space.

The big challenge is to work not only for the better of our organisation, but also for the better of our world. There is always room for improvement. For example, today we use ecological dye in some collections but over time our aim is to only use vegetable dyes. An ever-increasing portion of the market demands increased transparency and sustainability from the fashion industry and it will have no other choice but to change, to reflect the real cost of materials and production and with this, a tremendous change in consumption patterns will take place. Today a consumer may have to take some time to research brands that are genuine in their commitment to sustainable production. However, the demand for these types of products and brands will be increasing and the communication and tools to help the consumer choose less but better will be vastly improved. The responsibility to make the change is ours, and it's now.

ADVICE TO THE BRAVE

Be creative, hardworking, and surround yourself with good role models to help find the right balance between efficiency, handmade, and profitability. And remain open to new demands and ideas to reshape your model.

CARLIE BALLARD

New South Wales, Australia | carlieballard.com

CREATIVE BEGINNINGS

In September 2008, while working in adventure travel, I journeyed out on an educational trek in the Everest region of Nepal. Being immersed in nature in this part of the world is raw and abundant with new experiences and visuals. There was plenty of time to think and focus while you trek one foot in front of the other up through the altitude. I came away with an unwavering emotion of needing to help and empower. The people of Nepal were some of the most caring, friendly, and happy I had experienced in my travels. As a western tourist I felt I was in a position to create change in some way for people living there or in other similar cultures and countries. The thought was, how can I harness their unique skills, and translate it to something the western community of consumers would want to buy, in order to support this community.

It wasn't until July 2012 that I finally launched Indigo Bazaar, an online platform selling brands from around the world with ethical values. Back then it was hard to find Australian labels designing sustainable garments that were fashionable. It was so exciting; I had no idea about having an online business at all, I just knew how I wanted the website to look and feel. At the time my message was very strong in highlighting how damaging the mainstream fashion scene is, how poorly workers are treated, and how people just have no idea about the journey of their garments to the shop floor. I held market stalls at a local organic farmers' market, which was invaluable to connect with people that were interested in this space. However, as it was 2012, before the Rana Plaza disaster had happened, I quickly learned that people then just wanted to buy a pretty dress, they didn't want to hear the horror stories of the unethical production of all their other fashion purchases.

I continued with Indigo Bazaar as a platform for another year or so, then through the Sustainable Fashion Australia Facebook group I met a wonderful woman called Penny. Penny had set up a small cut, make, and trim workshop/social enterprise in the city of Lucknow, India after her and her husband had spent three years there on another project. The workshop was specifically created to offer a safe environment for women in the nearby slums to come and work. They are illiterate, but intelligent and resourceful women who create the most beautiful embroidery. When Penny and I met, our values and visions aligned and I was inspired to leap into designing my own collections. The workshop had no minimums either, so it was a really nurturing space for a start-up business to find its feet.

MOTIVATION

I would never have had a fashion brand if it wasn't a living and breathing extension of my values and beliefs. I loved fashion, but not enough that I wanted to create just another clothing brand, so I waited until the time was right in my career and I had found all the pieces of the puzzle to create a business. I kept myself up all night planning, so I knew I had to start it and get it out of my system! I really love what I do, but I think you have to in this space. It's challenging on so many fronts.

In 2013 when I started working on the label there weren't as many accessible and sustainable fibres to choose from as there are today. Plus, anyone offering beautiful sustainable fibres wanted at least a 1,000 metre minimum order, and when you're an independent designer, that just isn't an option! So, Penny helped me source handwoven ikat patterned fabric which had 25 metre minimums. I loved the fabric and prints and the minimums were manageable for my budget. And that was the beginning of my journey with handloom!

I initially purchased from existing stocks and collaborated with a pattern maker from Sydney to create my first four pieces for the collection. The Traveller trousers were my very first product. People loved the prints and appreciated that they were created on a handloom. They connected with the softness of the fabric and the durability of the weave. I had customers tell me they had people chase them across the street to ask them where they got their trousers from! It was a nice feeling, and from there I was given the confidence to persist.

> "As soon as people can tell that the pattern on our pieces isn't a print, it sparks conversation"

Since the launch of the label, the only other fabric I have used in the collection is an organic machine-loomed voile. I love the creativity the restriction of using just one fabric brings. The craft of handloom speaks to my art background, and the process of creating the fabric is an artisan process – a skill heavily passed down from generation to generation. I connect with handloom on so many levels. The history of the craft is one of the elements of the business I am most passionate about. I'm a sentimental being and I want to play my part in ensuring this craft remains relevant across cultures and generations. It's important to ensure it is aesthetically relevant so I feel that is what my role is – transforming handloom into wearable garments for our culture and society. As soon as people can tell that the pattern on our pieces isn't a print, it sparks conversation. The beauty is so visible. And it's these questions that allow the act of wearing to strike up meaningful conversations, create awareness, and share the importance of this traditional craft.

Traditional ikat can be traced back to the fifth century in India and likely around similar times in Central Asia and South East Asia as well. Traditionally it was a sign of great wealth and prestige and is still used throughout India for wedding ceremonies. It was Ghandi who saw the need for the people of India to clothe themselves through hand spinning and weaving their own fabric. He saw the increase in imported fabrics, and was determined to ensure that every home had a handloom so people could clothe themselves from fibre grown in India. The beauty of handloom is that it is powered by human energy and skill, not power which is reliant on infrastructure and money. His vision is still discussed widely today.

From a social aspect, engaging in traditional handloom allows artisans to remain in their villages with their families rather than moving away to the city for work. Using their skills brings so much value to my brand and I adore communicating this to our customers; it makes me so proud to have taken this path. I love that we use a traditional age-old technique in a more contemporary garment to appeal to our market which ultimately not only increases awareness of this beautiful craft, but helps to elevate it and keep the technique alive. Co-creating with artisans is a beautiful thing. They live and breathe their craft and we can learn so much from them.

Artisans are the second largest employment sector globally so they are such a cultural asset to be celebrated. I feel it's my role as a designer to communicate their value through our business. The more younger generations of Indian men and women follow on from their parents, the more progressive and successful the industry can be.

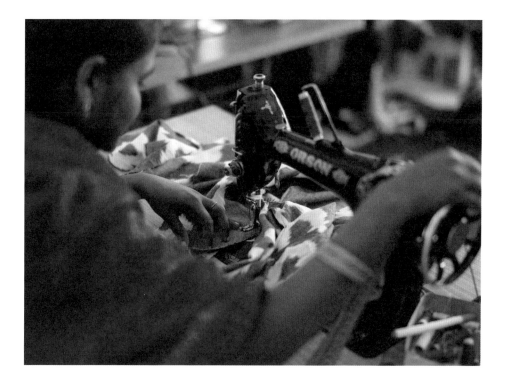

"Co-creating with artisans is a beautiful thing. They live and breathe their craft and we can learn so much from them"

PRACTICALITIES

I find my style is quite practical, but I definitely add a twist to create our signature designs. Inevitably I'm influenced by my own needs and expectations of clothing, and since having children I have created more styles with buttons to allow for breastfeeding. I think my customer is coming along on this journey with me, their needs are changing like mine, and I enjoy this concept of the brand evolving. The Carlie Ballard muse is a dreamer, a make-believer, an adventurer forging her own path. She is confident yet playful, and a woman who never stops exploring. Her style is sophisticated yet eclectic and rich in visual stories.

> "We are acutely aware of the importance to people and planet, and to our children's future"

We make a women's collection twice a year. Our collections seem to appeal to a wide audience of women of all ages, which I love. My intention with each collection is to create designs that are wearable every day. Some are bolder than others, often dictated by the lovely patterns. The part I enjoy the most is designing and coming up with new collections. Immersing myself in the concept and inspiration for each collection is a beautiful research stage. It's always nerve-wracking waiting for the post and opening up the samples, hoping I've put all the pieces together technically and aesthetically. I also adore the people that work in this space – it feels as though we all want to elevate each other and help the collective movement. We are acutely aware of the importance to people and planet, and to our children's future.

EMPOWERMENT AND EVOLUTION

Sustainability is our complete existence. It's our *why*. We started because we want to empower people, create change and advocate for change in the fashion industry. I have an innate desire to change how things are done in the realm of fashion and to inspire change, which is why a group of us here in Sydney started Clean Cut Fashion – to inspire change to the Australian fashion landscape.

When I first started the brand, sustainability to me was very much about sustainable livelihoods, fair pay for a fair day's work and creating clothing in a space that was safe, fair, and supportive. As my time in this space evolved, I became increasingly interested in the relationship we have with clothing – how it defines an era, narrates our style on a daily basis, and how we can truly connect with a garment once we understand the story and path it took to get to our wardrobe. Communicating the value of a garment and the generations of artisan knowledge and quality of our pieces is also a passion of mine.

Zenana Women, our cut, make and trim workshop is a social enterprise created to empower the women it set out to employ. The workshop follows the ten standards set out by the World Fair Trade Association to provide a fair workplace for its employees and goes above and beyond in terms of emotional support to many of the staff, including childcare, financial assistance, and extended leave.

> "... our cut, make and trim workshop is a social enterprise created to empower the women it set out to employ"

Each garment is made by one person, our workshop doesn't do piecework, but it also means they have the knowledge to complete a whole garment from start to finish, which is often rare in India. We make small collections, and re-make more units as demand requires to reduce deadstock. We use our scraps for things such as scrunchies and drawstring bags, and we're also about to launch swatch packs for people to purchase and create their own things with our fabrics! We also package our garments in packaging that degrades in 180 days and leaves no trace, and our mailers are compostable in your home compost bin.

We work with artisan handweavers so that our fabrics also hold great value in our supply chain and finished product. Handwoven fabric has an energy about it. It's been created by hand and human energy, not with electricity. Handwoven ikat involves a time-consuming process of tying and dyeing the material, sometimes multiple times depending on how many colours are in the print. So, we do need to be well ahead of the fashion calendar to ensure we can meet deadlines. Communicating with India can often be challenging and because handloom is done in village cooperatives, we often get marks on our fabrics because they are not made in big factories that are squeaky clean. So, we pre-wash and pre-shrink all our fabric before they are made into garments. Often handloomed fabric has slubs through the fabric which is a beautiful organic part of the process, and sometimes even pieces of the cotton shell are woven into the fabric!

WORKSPACE

My workspace is in our home on the coast of New South Wales, Australia. I'm immersed in all my fabrics, books, and garments and it's my little happy place. It allows me to pop in any time to work on things and pack orders, and allows great flexible working hours as a mum with two small children.

My design process starts often by removing myself from my workshop and either going to sit in nature or flicking through home styling or architecture books. An idea always circulates well before it's time to begin drawing.

The people I work with are my key tools. Penny the workshop director and I work very closely daily on production, pattern making, and construction of garments. Because I don't have formal fashion design training, I lean on Penny for any technical advice. I also work with a pattern maker for certain new pieces, but we often adapt existing pattern blocks that have worked really well to ensure our fit has continuity each season.

When we have put together a design and lifted it off the piece of paper, Masterji, the head tailor in India will create a toile for me. They're sent over to me and I pin, and measure until we have the right fit and aesthetic I envisioned. Sometimes we get it right first time, but often things will require tweaking before the sampling stage.

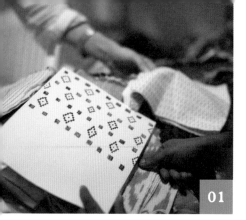

IKAT WEAVING PROCESS OVERVIEW

01 To begin the making process, I first share my designs with the team of artisans to discuss the techniques that may be required.

02 To begin the making process, and prepare the base for the ikat fabric, yarn is first separated from the spools using a warping mill.

03 One of the artisans then manually stretches the yarn into 25m lengths, ready for tying.

04 Next, the artisan draws the chosen ikat design onto the yarn to ensure the tying (banding) is done accurately. This is the unique element of

the ikat process – the design is created through the tie and dyeing before weaving has begun.

05 An artisan ties together groups of yarn using elastic banding. The banding creates a resist so that when dyed, the dye only colours the exposed sections of the yarn. The yarn is dip-dyed many times into a dye pot, washed and then put out to dry. For single ikat only the warp is dyed, while the weft is a single colour yarn.

06 The weft yarn is spooled in preparation for weaving. To develop a double ikat pattern, both the warp and weft are dyed – this type of

05

06

07

ikat requires great skill, as both warp and weft patterns need to be created through the tie and dye process before weaving. Once at the weaving stage, the weaver meticulously aligns the design with the correctly dyed sections of the yarn.

07 Once weaved, the beautiful ikat patterned fabric is then sewn together using dressmaking techniques to create a variety of different garments.

"When we have put together a design and lifted it off the piece of paper, Masterji, the head tailor in India will create a toile for me. They're sent over to me and I pin, and measure until we have the right fit and aesthetic I envisioned"

THE DAY-TO-DAY

On my work days I drop my children at day-care and head straight to my local cafe. I look forward to this time to go through Instagram and emails briefly and plan my day ahead. My to-do lists are always long, but I feel so grateful to be able to sit in my home office and plough through the tasks uninterrupted. My work days are sacred and I really try to not plan anything else on these days. I just get in my zone and focus. In the afternoon I'll always have orders to pack and take to the post office before I head to pick up the kids again. I love missing them and seeing them at the end of the day!

Initially we sold our garments at markets, then moved onto online, wholesale, and drop shipping, and also had our own brick and mortar store for four years. Social media has been a huge opportunity for our brand. Connecting with people and answering their questions, but also inspiring them has been a huge business advantage for us. It can be very exhausting at times though and I often find myself addicted to checking it in case I've missed something important! But overall social media such as Facebook, Instagram, and Pinterest, as well as blogs sends us a lot of online traffic.

Our business has grown and our customers now really respond to the ikat prints. Whenever we post about our process on social media people just adore seeing the journey of the garment. It gives it so much more value and narrative. It's allowed me to really tell the story to our customers and capture their attention in a way that is restrictive with print. The ability to pinpoint people who have commented or just viewed and interacted with the brand is a huge asset when building a brand.

CONNECT WITH YOUR MAKERS

Before you become client facing, ensure you have spent the time and money finding the right people to create your brand and aesthetic. This side of the business is so very important. Create meaningful relationships with your makers and experience how they work – this allows you to understand and tell their story with transparency and sincerity.

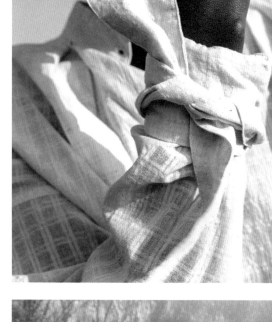

CONSCIOUS CONCEPTS

Fashion for us is very much about the storytelling of our collections and communicating their journey to our customers. For example, our summer 2019/20 collection is inspired by romantic poets from the late 18th and 19th century such as John Keats. Our collections started out purely ikat, but as the collections progressed, we introduced plain weaves as well to ensure we captured a market that wasn't interested in ikat. But now we have realised that ikat truly is our signature, so our next collection features our beloved ikat again! We try to work with colours that are current where possible, but as we work ahead of the fashion calendar, that can be difficult, so sometimes we just roll with our own colour palettes.

Innovation in fabric production is very exciting in this space, however we just watch and enjoy it from afar and will always be completely devoted to working with handloom, to ensure we stay true to our values of supporting and uplifting the artisans and garment workers that we have worked with for a long time. Innovation for us is communicating that this age-old handloom technique is still relevant in a society of fast fashion. And it is important to know who made your garment – something that used to be normal thirty years ago before mass-production grew.

From the inception of the business we have been price point conscious, because we were aware that people's perception is that ethical clothing is expensive. So, from the design stage we consider the price point balance between fabric, labour costs, and garment details to ensure we create a product that is affordable for the customer we have cultivated. As a slow fashion business, we would never consider outsourcing cheaply to be able to sell more for less. We would rather work with more artisans to grow the business, rather than provide an inferior product. We have a very holistic approach to sustainability in business.

Although I am slightly envious of the resources of big sustainable brands, I am inspired, and encouraged that sustainable fashion brands have found success because it means more and more people are conscious about what they buy and who makes their garments! Although there are cheaper high-street alternatives to our products, we accept that there always will be, and instead try to focus on our craft and try to blinker ourselves from these brands.

"Innovation for us is communicating that this age-old handloom technique is still relevant in a society of fast fashion"

THE FUTURE

In the near future, we will be changing some of our fabric suppliers and working with a wider range of artisans to expand our handloom offerings. Plus, I'm very excited to be working on a new baby and toddler collection. We are also very keen to start the process of getting B Corporation certified. It can be hard to get certifications when you work with artisans as often there are expensive annual subscriptions which artisans don't see the value in. We would also like to launch a buy back second-hand store of Carlie Ballard pieces. By offering people who return our garments once they are finished with them, a discount on new collection pieces, we would be helping to keep them in circulation.

From when I began my research in 2008 there has been a huge amount of change. I struggled to find anything from Australia that was promoted as ethical or consciously sourced, and now it feels like the groundswell is enormous! The conversation has grown from simply talking about using organic materials, to a call for a more circular economy, and now the modern citizen wants to be more conscious of their purchasing decisions. Now you can return garments to brands to be resold, rent garments for temporary use, or trace the provenance of a garment and discover who made it. It's powerful.

We are also seeing all different types of fabric technology such as rPET, pineapple, orange, and milk fibres that are actually viable, and finding that some technologies have their disadvantages such as rPET which has created a whole new area for researching how to stop microfibres leaking into the oceans through washing machine technology. I think what I love about handloom is that it's not re-inventing a skill, it's co-creating with the artisans to empower them and to ensure they realise their craft is still relevant, and important. It is our job as designers to ensure we can tell their story and create that enormous value proposition to the customer; to romanticise the beauty of handloom and turn it into wearable art.

In order to make a change, high-street brands need to stop making so many clothes, especially garments that are designed to last only a few wears. I believe the fashion industry as a whole needs to phase out nylon and polyester fabrics and introduce more sustainable fibres. Consumers have to do their part by asking questions and demanding better fabrics and better labour conditions, but ultimately it is the responsibility of the businesses and designers to change the products they create and to consider their social and environmental impact.

WHAT'S YOUR *WHY*?

As a designer, take time to understand where your values and passions lie – is it in artisan and craft sustainability, or is it ensuring the cotton is organic, or are you wanting to make sure that disadvantaged people make your garments? Navigating this path is a challenging journey for a designer as well as a consumer. Once you figure out your *why*, you will understand your brand.

SHOEMAKING

Traditionally shoes were crafted individually by hand by master craftspeople, but since its commercialisation in the mid-18th century, footwear has become largely mass-produced. Shoemakers craft shoes of a wide range of different styles and shapes, from a variety of materials, including leather, wood, rubber, plastic, or plant-based fabrics. The sole is stitched to the upper parts to form the basis of a shoe.

- -

"We love finding the balance between beautiful, useful, and sustainable, and connecting people with the stories of their shoes"

Joanna Hamer, Juta Shoes

JUTA SHOES

Joanna Hamer and Sabeha Miah
London, UK | jutashoes.com

CREATIVE BEGINNINGS

Juta Shoes was born in Bethnal Green, out of the talents and needs of the local community. In East London, there's a large community of women with amazing craft skills but without access to employment in the creative sector. The past few years have seen such a surge of independent craft enterprises, but barriers to work such as social isolation, caring responsibilities, lack of experience or confidence, as well as speaking English as a second language, mean that women from BAME (black, Asian and minority ethnic) refugee and migrant communities, are underrepresented in this sector.

However, there is a huge amount of talent and skill in our community, in everything from embroidery, sewing, and crochet to catering, and creative employment offers such a unique opportunity for expression, flexibility, support, and community. Juta Shoes is a community of women who have been unemployed or underemployed on low incomes, supporting themselves and each other through craft.

The Juta Shoes team makes handcrafted bespoke leather espadrilles, from eco-friendly jute soles and leather reclaimed from a local factory as well as reclaimed upholstery offcuts. We're all self-taught, and we teach others to make their own shoes in our public shoemaking workshops.

We enjoy creating and teaching others to make wearable items because of the sense of pride and responsibility that comes from making something that people will use and rely on in their daily lives. We love finding the balance between beautiful, useful, and sustainable, and connecting people with the stories of their shoes.

WHY MAKE?

For new makers, before you start we think it's really important to take time to think about why you're making what you're making – how does it make you feel, who needs it, what resources does it use, and what problems does it solve?

MOTIVATION

Sustainability is central to everything we do. All our leather is reclaimed, and we try to use natural and biodegradable materials in all our designs. In Bangladesh, where many of the Juta makers are from, nothing is thrown away. Everything has a second life and a use. Old cotton saris are turned into kantha blankets, potato sacks are woven into rugs, and gourds are dried out and carved into bowls. We are also inspired by the history of craft in our own lives. Each of our mothers made things and passed down skills in knitting, quilting, sewing, carving, or weaving. We've all gone through the cycle of growing up thinking we wouldn't do what our mothers did, but then realising how much value and heritage were in their crafts and asking them to teach us what they know.

The shoe industry in particular hasn't got a great reputation for sustainability as most often the glues that are used are toxic to workers and the environment, and mean that the shoes can't be recycled at the end of their life. We're trying to work against this however we can, through our products as well as through conversations and workshops.

There's a huge sense of community within our studio, but also with other makers that we work with, from our stockists and collaborators to other creative enterprises in our community. We have definitely seen an elevation in the appreciation of handmade crafts in recent years. We find that more people go out of their way to look for products made locally, where they can meet the artisans and trace the materials throughout the whole supply chain. At Juta Shoes, the whole process of making takes place in our studio, and anyone can come and watch, or learn to make their own.

For us, making is therapeutic – not just the slow, meditative process of repeating stitches, but also the celebration and pleasure in the finished product. We bounce off each other with creative ideas, patterns and techniques, defining and refining new designs. Craft motivates us, connects us, and increases our self-esteem. We also see how it inspires others when they see us making, and improves their well-being as well as our own. We encourage each other and take pride in each other's accomplishments. Especially if you begin thinking, "I could never make that," or "I could never teach this skill to someone else," when you achieve it, it's great for your self-esteem. Something that you have hand-made for someone has importance and value like nothing else – it shows them that they matter, and that they're connected to the person who made it.

"Making is therapeutic – not just the slow, meditative process of repeating stitches, but also the celebration and pleasure in the finished product"

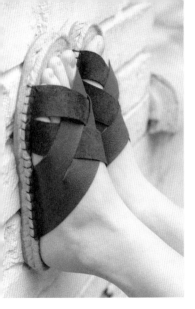

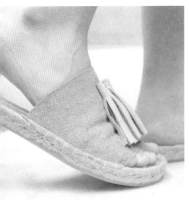

THE STUDIO

Our studio is based at St Margaret's House, a local charity and community centre supporting well-being in Bethnal Green. We're based in The Create Place, a multipurpose arts space. We share the space with other arts and craft projects, which we absolutely love – there's often life drawing, jewellery making, sewing classes, or community groups having tea and biscuits in the space. We also share storage with the charity shop next door, which means that if they get a donation of fabric they can't use we can often use it for sample shoes.

We hold our workshops in the downstairs room at The Create Place, with a big window facing the street. It means that people often stop by and look at what we're doing, and sometimes come in to ask questions or chat. That window is often our best recruitment method for new makers! It's also sunny and bright, which makes the whole studio glow. We have a lovely kitchen at the back and a small enclosed garden that's flooded with sunlight in the afternoon, giving us a nice place to relax and a perfect spot to take photos of our just-finished shoes.

The key tools that we use for our shoemaking are scissors, pliers, needles, pins, and thread. In traditional shoemaking, you wouldn't cut the leather with scissors, but for our espadrilles we use softer leather than you would for boots or brogues, and we've found that scissors are friendlier for new shoemakers than scalpels or knives. We use special pins, 0.6 x 32 mm in size, that are just the right strength and diameter to push through the leather without bruising your fingers. Then we sew with waxed linen thread, which is very strong, and special glover's needles.

We use miniature needle nose pliers (commonly used in jewellery making) to pull the needle through the sole and leather. These tools are very special to us: they're portable, but very strong, and they allow anyone to turn a complicated movement into a simple seamless motion.

ESPADRILLES PROCESS OVERVIEW

01 The first step of making a shoe is to choose the size and pattern. We have several different styles, and eleven sizes. Then we choose the pieces of leather – sometimes we mix and match a variety of colours, or flip the leather over to use the suede side.

02 We lay the leather out on the table and examine it for imperfections and stretch. Because our leather is all reclaimed from offcuts, there are often marks, lines, or cuts in the leather, and sometimes we get pieces with too much or too little stretch for our styles. Those pieces are saved for other accessories.

03 When we've chosen the piece we'll use, we lay the pattern down on top of it and draw around it with either a gel pen or chalk. We can also adjust the pattern here for people with wide or narrow feet, especially on workshops.

04 Then we cut the pattern out with our very sharp Fiskars scissors, and clean off any remaining pen or chalk marks with a damp cloth.

05 Once we have the pattern and sole, we pin them together in the shape of the shoe. We teach people on our workshops to always pin the leather to the edge of the sole to ensure the right sizing, and to pin inwards at an angle for a secure hold.

06 Then we start sewing using a sharp glover's needle, waxed linen thread, and our needle nose pliers to pull the needle through the sole and leather.

"There is a huge amount of talent and skill in our community, in everything from embroidery, sewing, and crochet to catering, and creative employment offers such a unique opportunity for expression, flexibility, support, and community"

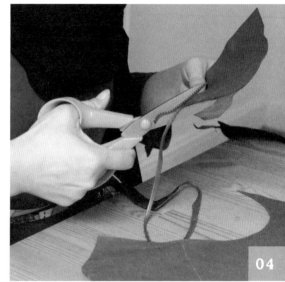

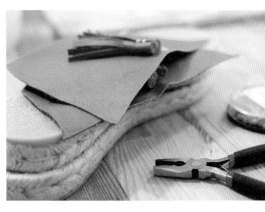

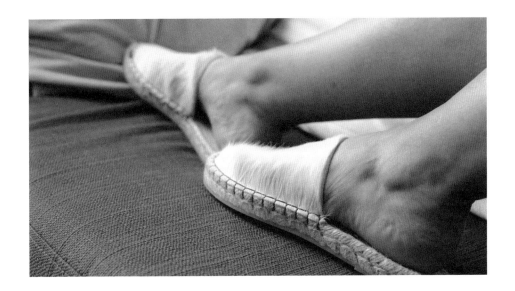

CRAFTING A BUSINESS

We started off simply making shoes, but then people started asking if they could join us at our studio and learn to make their own. We started offering shoemaking workshops, and they have taken off as our main income stream. We find that people very much enjoy the experience of selecting their leathers, making small adjustments, and sewing their own shoes from scratch.

We mainly sell our shoes and workshops through our website, as well as through craft workshop platforms and to companies. We've had such success working with partners such as Daylesford Farm, WeWork, AirBnB, and Anthropologie to bring our workshops to new audiences, and running team crafts days for companies.

An average day at the Juta Shoes studio starts after the children are dropped off at school, when we break out the cups of tea and biscuits. We'll look at the orders we've had in that week, and take out our equipment from the cupboards. If we have new trainees, they'll be working on their first sample shoes, overseen by experienced makers, or learning how to teach a workshop. We might have an external designer or stockist come in to talk about a product they're working with us to develop, or someone from another local social enterprise or charity to talk about referrals or extra support services. Then in the afternoon there'll be plenty of email answering and phone calls for the directors, future planning, and financial modelling.

Everyone at Juta works part-time or flexibly. We make sure the work fits around our lives and always pays us the London Living Wage. As a small and new company, this means that there isn't yet enough work for us to work full-time, so many of us juggle other commitments or work on the side. It can be difficult to make a craft business work financially, but there are creative ways to find different customers and broaden the possible streams of income. For example, we often give talks about social enterprise, craft, and women's empowerment for organisations around London.

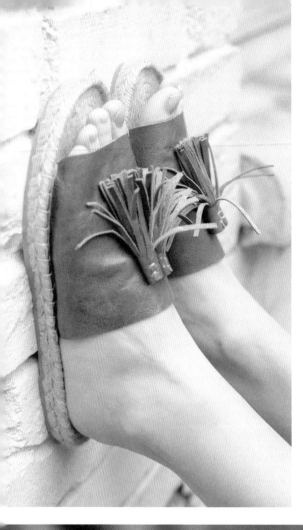

MODERN YET TRADITIONAL

We're a very modern and a very traditional business. Things are done slowly, by hand, in traditional ways, but we also love social media for how it connects us to our audience and shares our message. We don't follow trends and are deeply against fast fashion, but we love working with individual customers to design and tweak their own perfect bespoke shoes.

It's really important to us that our making is done by us, in our community. We don't think we compete against other brands – we're each doing something different, and our customers choose us because of our ethics and social mission. If they choose another company for the same reason, then the same purpose has been achieved.

THE FUTURE

We have big hopes for the future – we want to keep making shoes and teaching workshops, reclaiming leather, and taking on more makers in our community. We'd love to develop more products and workshops, drawing on our heritage crafts, and connect more charities, businesses, and social enterprises in London. Products connect people, those who make it and those who wear it, and the wider world, and craft is so important to keep these relationships alive.

For our industry, it's about being more responsible and listening more. Small companies like us are getting together, making more noise, and demonstrating that another way is possible. Consumers are realising that they can ask for more, and that their choices can make a difference, especially when amplified and connected globally.

"Our customers choose us because of our ethics and social mission. If they choose another company for the same reason, then the same purpose has been achieved"

GARMENT MAKING

Garment making, also known as dressmaking and tailoring, involves sewing component pieces of fabric together to assemble a wearable item of clothing. The parts of the garment are first cut out of the fabric using a paper pattern and scissors before being sewn together by hand or machine.

- -

"I want to create clothing that people feel like themselves in – clothing that works for many different body shapes and sizes to move away from the unethical fast-moving fashion of the high street"

Deva O'Neill, Phaedra Clothing

PHAEDRA CLOTHING

Deva O'Neill
Norwich, UK | phaedraclothing.co.uk

CREATIVE BEGINNINGS

As a tall woman, I was constantly scouring charity shops and the high street for simple dresses that fitted me. I had a strong idea of what I wanted – a very simple style, comfortable to wear, in muted colours – but could never find it. I had a lightbulb moment – why not try and sew my own clothes? And from that thought, my obsession with making clothes was born. I was able to turn this skill into a way to reach my long-term goal of being financially independent and self-employed. It was always important to me that my business grew organically, without debt or major overheads. I took the leap and found myself a studio space while working part-time as a baker to pay the bills, and slowly built up an online presence and customer base until I felt I could justify being fully self-employed. It's now five years on, and I make dozens of designs, in many different colours to order.

> "I aim to sew garments that will last, and create long and happy relationships between wearer and worn"

The collection is inspired by Japanese design and workwear, which combines attention to detail with practical, everyday wear. I want to create clothing that people feel like themselves in – clothing that works for all different body shapes and sizes, to move away from the unethical fast-moving fashion of the high street. I aim to sew garments that will last, and create long and happy relationships between wearer and worn.

MOTIVATION

Choosing the slower, more considered way in all aspects of my life brings me great satisfaction and pride, and holds me directly responsible for my actions. I like to leave as gentle a mark on the resources of the world as possible – I'm a vegan, grow my own food, choose to use eco-friendly and organic products, and practise zero-waste living. Mirroring these values when it came to my craft felt like a natural evolution.

Working with cloth is very gratifying. To hold such rich colours and textures in my hands all day is a very grounding experience. I often find myself drifting off into simple happiness when I'm sewing, and to have a finished object that holds so much potential of use and wear at the end of the day is empowering and rewarding.

I see my craft as a political act. Turning my back on fast fashion meant finding so many more facets to clothing that had rarely crossed my mind when I was entrenched in a quick-buy attitude, namely the extent that the clothes industry is affecting our planet. I choose to use natural fabrics; linen in particular, which uses much less water and pesticides than most fabric processing. Every part of the flax plant is used in production, and it biodegrades, leaving no trace of man-made fibres that are harmful to our eco-systems. I use British-made corozo nut buttons and notions, and buy from textile mills in the UK. Buying directly from the source creates transparency, and a sense of community with those who make the fabric. I can be sure of the quality of the cloth, and of the rights of the workers in these factories. The direct link holds myself and others accountable. I use eco-certified dyes, and send all larger fabric scraps to quilters and hobbyists in an effort to be zero-waste. Smaller pieces and threads go into making cushions and pouffes.

> "I often find myself drifting off into simple happiness when I'm sewing, and to have a finished object that holds so much potential of use and wear at the end of the day is empowering and rewarding"

Alongside this, I love to celebrate the individuality of our bodies. Most high street brands don't cater for vastly different body sizes and shapes, and so making garments to order is part of my core manifesto. I want to create clothes that are comfortable, clothes that are elegant and flattering, as well as clothes that can go out on adventures with their wearers. Customers can choose to customise the length of their garments, and choose from a variety of sizes to be sure they have the fit they want. It leads to a long and happy relationship between garment and wearer that turns its back on the throwaway fast fashion culture that is the norm in the UK.

I have seen a definite shift in how people approach sustainability in their own lives over the last few years, and more and more people are choosing to invest in pieces that will last, from smaller clothes brands, and appreciating the work that goes into everyday items instead of taking them for granted. It's a response to fast-paced consumerism, a more inward-looking decision that celebrates human rather than machine, community over global conglomerates, appreciation over competition.

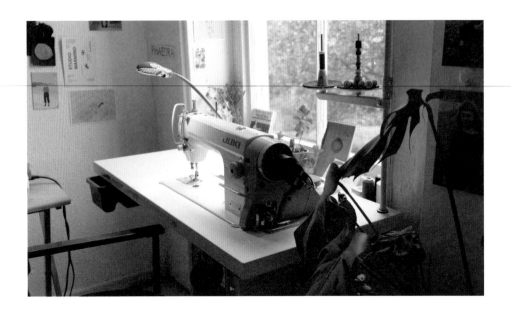

STUDIO

My studio is part of a network of rooms in an old shoe-making factory in Norwich, a grand and dilapidated red-brick building with echoes of its old industry. I sit sewing at a large window, looking out over a cherry tree. I design, cut, and sew all my garments from here with an industrial sewing machine, an ironing board, and a large fabric cutting table. Rolls of fabric are propped in one corner, and huge lever-arch files house all of my clothes patterns. Folded piles of fabric for future projects are shelved with my overlocker machine.

> "It's a place where my projects can lay undisturbed – a place
> solely for craft and play, an extension of my creative mind"

I'm inspired by painters, poems, the outdoors, and architecture, and so the walls and windowsills are set with postcards, plants, and found objects – it keeps my inspiration flowing. Having a studio is so important to me. It's a place where my projects can lay undisturbed – a place solely for craft and play, an extension of my creative mind.

STAY TRUE

My advice to someone considering this line of work is to stay true to your own vision, whatever that may be, and try not compare yourself to others. Stay strong in your integrity, never compromise your morals, and value your time and craft.

LINEN DRESS PROCESS OVERVIEW

01 First, I lay out the fabric, pin the pattern in place, and cut out the design. I make the most of every inch of fabric, while following the grain of the linen.

02 I pin and sew the shoulder seams to create the main bodice of the garment. Linen is springy and the weave is rough, so pinning is important to keep the seams straight.

03 Overlocking the seams is the next step. The overlocker trims the seam with a sharp blade, and sews with four different threads to reinforce the seam. A third line of overstitching adds longevity to the garment.

04 I attach the pockets to the sides of the skirt fabric. Pockets feature in nearly every style I make, they're very important to me. I find shop-bought garments rarely have deep enough pockets, particularly in women's clothing.

05 I pleat the skirt and attach it to the bodice. Pleats help to create a roomier skirt for more freedom of movement. I offer a customisation service that means any skirt can be lengthened or shortened for free.

06 After sewing down the side seams of the garment, I pin the sleeves in place and sew them on. Many of my garments feature a drop sleeve, the kind you might find on a kimono.

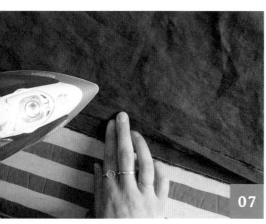

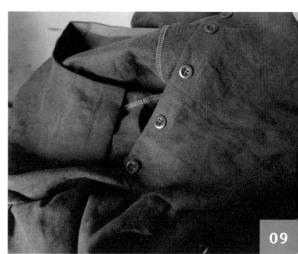

Which means the sleeve begins on your upper arm rather than on the shoulder, and drapes nicely on all shoulder-types.

07 I hem the bottom of the dress and the sleeves. I draw out the seam allowance and iron it in place, adding pins as I go to keep the fabric in line. I find this task the most satisfying!

08 I attach the bias binding to the neck, first sewing it in place, then ironing and folding it back into the underside of the garment. Fabric cut on the bias stretches well around corners, and bias binding can be used to create a very sleek neckline.

09 I attach buttons using a domestic sewing machine. First the place where the button will sit is marked on the fabric, and then the button is sewn on. Then I mark the buttonholes and the machine sews these too. I use corozo nut buttons that are manufactured in the UK in a revived industry dating back to the 1850's. Most of the same techniques are used, and in some cases the original machinery.

THE DAY-TO-DAY

On an average day, I walk to the studio along the river. I write new orders in my ledger, and an action plan for the day ahead. I usually make two or three garments in a day while listening to podcasts and drinking plenty of tea. I prefer to sew different styles and colours rather than batch-make a certain item, as it gives a little variety to my making. But it's not all sewing – I'm currently working on extending my size range, and spend time drawing up new designs, updating my online shop, and answering emails. I also make sure to set aside time every week for personal projects, such as fixing my own clothing. I very much follow the make-do-and-mend philosophy.

I predominantly sell my garments online through my website, but I also open my studio once every few months to meet customers face-to-face, which I love to do. It's important to me to make real connections with my customers, to make the experience of buying a happy and considered one. Social media, particularly Instagram, has played a huge part in the success of my business. I send garments worldwide, and it's wonderful to think of garments that have been created by me in places I have never been. I have also met many other makers and a genuine, like-minded supportive community.

"It's important to me to make real connections with my customers, to make the experience of buying a happy and considered one"

Being self-employed can be challenging, there's always work to be done and a list of things to be ticked off, but it's the most empowering experience. To only be answerable to yourself, to find your own workflow, and to have the space and time to craft whatever you feel like is a liberation and a luxury.

SUSTAINING CREATIVITY

Staying true to my own vision is the most important thing for my creativity. It's very easy to be influenced by others around you in this digital age where perception of creative success is directly linked to public reactions on social media. My creativity is more important, it's a gentle thing that is cultivated and treated with care, and so I work at my own pace. I don't pander to current trends; I only offer new garments after my own personal bursts of inspiration and ensuing productivity, rather than by the season.

I don't worry about competing with larger brands; there is a growing movement towards meaningful choice in fashion as the public grows more aware of the price we pay for large-scale clothes making, on both workers' rights and the environment. More people are choosing to buy from smaller, ethical brands which is heartening. I price my garments fairly in direct response to the time taken to make a garment, and its costs involved. I'm under no illusion as to the fact that not everyone can afford to buy ethical all the time, but I want to make ethical clothing as accessible as I can while valuing my own time and being uncompromising on quality.

THE FUTURE

As Phaedra moves into the future, I would love to have a larger studio, and be able to invite others to work alongside me, perhaps a team of three or four. I would never want to lose the intimacy that I have with all levels of production and aspects of the business, as I enjoy it all equally. Imminently, I'm exploring more British textiles and other sustainable fabrics such as hemp and wool, and looking deeper at the tradition of milling and clothes-making in the UK. I'm also interested in delving into the world of natural dyes, as it gives me great joy to continue to make closer connections with the land around me through colour, and to be able to forage from my own landscapes.

> "We as consumers hold the power together to change the direction"

I hope in the future to see more consumers holding larger companies accountable for their wasteful actions and putting pressure on them to change. It's impossible to avoid fast fashion all together, and so calling out those companies and asking for more transparency in their production is a step forward. We as consumers hold the power together to change the direction.

A move towards decreased cotton production, less pesticides and herbicides, and a focus on sustainable crops such as hemp and linen would have a huge impact on global water use and soil care. I would also love to see schools offering lessons on more traditional crafts such as dressmaking again, which has all but dropped off the curriculum. An educated person is empowered to make their own choices.

> "... creating connections with the people who make your clothes and homewares can forge great meaning and purpose to the objects you choose to surround yourself with"

My advice to consumers looking to buy more sustainably would be to choose your purchases carefully. Save up for a little longer and buy something that is of quality, that will last. Consider which garments you truly need, which bring you happiness, what colours you like, and choose new additions with consideration. Creating a capsule wardrobe is a great way to do this. And remember that not everything has to be bought. Use what you have, borrow, swap, thrift, or make before you take the leap to buy. When the time is right to buy, creating connections with the people who make your clothes and homewares can forge great meaning and purpose to the objects you choose to surround yourself with.

GROVE & CO.

Ben Martin and Tristan Evans
London, UK | groveand.co

- -

CREATIVE BEGINNINGS

Grove & Co. all started on a trip to Paris. While walking around fashionable areas such as the Marais, visiting different shops and looking to buy some nice shirts, we really struggled to find anything that wasn't a mass-produced, ubiquitous shirt. There were plenty of big-name brands, but even when we sought out smaller brands, we found that they didn't offer the quality or style we were looking for. So, we decided that we would start a business together crafting shirts. And that was it, that was the decision to get going.

Tristan's sister Joss is a pattern maker, so we worked with her on the design of our first shirt. Developing the pattern for our very first shirt was a long process, because neither of us have formal training in fashion – our backgrounds are in architecture and environmental law, so shirtmaking was a whole new area for us to learn. We are both passionate about getting into the intricate details of things, so we spent a year just trying to find out everything we could about shirts.

The key question with any business or opportunity that you have to ask yourself is "What can I bring that is unique to the market?" and for us it's our take on the men's shirt. There are hundreds of shirts out there, but it's our individual take, and all the features that we've put into our shirt that makes ours stand apart. Among the millennial generation, I believe there's a real feeling of "I'm not just defined by my job, I can also do these multiple things rather than just a person who does this job". Running Grove & Co. alongside our day jobs gives us both a creative outlet.

GO FOR IT!

If you want to start a craft business, choose something you're passionate about, because you have to spend a lot of time learning and developing your skills and talking to people about it. Live by the old proverb, "the best time to plant the tree was twenty years ago, the second-best time is today", and just do it. There is always a sense of "It's not quite right because I'm busy", but actually if you just go for it, you'll find out very quickly if you have time to do it or not, or if you really care about it.

MOTIVATION

I've always had a very keen interest in men's tailoring. I find fashion's history and traditions absolutely fascinating. I love the way traditions evolve over time and can be changed by the actions of one person. For example, the rule of always leaving the bottom button of your waistcoat or jacket undone originated from one king being too large for his suits. One of the main details we take away from men's tailoring is the idea of "gentlemen's pleasures" – hidden details that only the wearer knows about. Having hidden fabrics on the inside of your jacket or under your collar, it's a small pleasure – something that only you know about, and it's just for you. These themes come through in our shirts – we try to take those traditional elements and update them. We also really like that there's more freedom in fashion and what people wear now; there are no strict rules any more.

We aim to take something classic and make it contemporary while retaining the character of the original piece. In that process we imbue the design with a little bit of history and update a timeless piece. For example, we added an additional piece of fabric along the bottom of the inside of our shirts because we thought it would reduce wear on the inside of the shirt and also help it keep its shape. Although we added that fabric for practical purposes, we thought, why not use some contrasting fabrics and the only person that actually is aware of that is the wearer, because when the shirt is buttoned up it would be hidden on the inside. It's those kinds of small touches that we get quite excited about. That's the joy of designer pieces; as a designer you can have that connection to the product and the wearer can see all the care and love that's gone into the design as well.

CHOOSE YOUR PARTNER WISELY

If you are going to set up a business with someone, make sure you know each other well enough and you can tell each other when they're not pulling their weight or they need to be doing something that they're not. Tristan and I mercilessly tell each other when we think the other one is doing something wrong.

We like to use a production method where we know we can put our hands on it and say "Right, we know this has come from here and we know we can go and visit our factory there". We have a good relationship with our manufacturer so we frequently visit our factory and spend the day there. The trust and relationship element are central to our business. It is grounding to know that you have that personal connection to the people who make your product and to be able to see the product being made. In the UK the incredible manufacturing industry we used to have seemed to have almost died out, but we are excited to see that there's some momentum gathering around "British made" – and we consider ourselves fortunate to be a part of it.

I love repairing my clothes, and most of my clothes are patched up in some way. I think it's really positive when you have more of a relationship with your clothes than just a buy-use-discard cycle. I love the fact that you can visibly see the kind of use garments have had over the years, and the lift that a simple repair can give them. We aim to build all of our products for life. The message we want to put forward is that you can have something and it can get damaged and it doesn't need to be thrown away – you can simply repair it and it'll gain some character. Our manufacturer guarantee is that if there is a fault with the stitching or a button has fallen off then it can be sent back to us to be repaired. We decided to offer a discount to customers who repair their Grove & Co. products themselves because we feel that if we can encourage one person to sew a button back on or repair the stitching on their shirt, and they think "Actually that wasn't too bad, I can repair all my clothes rather than throw them away", that seems like a really easy and positive way to do a small good in the world.

TIMELESS BRITISH DESIGN

We design and make men's shirts for life and the modern workplace. We keep our product range very simple. As well as our regular collared shirt, we make a mandarin-collared shirt and a turtle-neck top. The main materials we use are high-quality end-of-line fabrics. And there's two reasons for that, one is the sustainability element of reusing otherwise waste materials, and two is that the shirt becomes a limited-edition product. The editions we release really are limited because we can't just buy more of the materials. Once they're gone, they're gone.

To design our shirts, we took inspiration from classic British shirt designs but wanted to give them a fresh twist, so we incorporated small contemporary design features, including curved collars, tortoiseshell buttons, and other small details which make the shirt stand out in the right way. We're big ones for constantly refining and reiterating our designs and ideas. Rather than just saying "We'll make a shirt this season, throw everything out and start again", we're constantly improving our existing designs.

When we first began Grove & Co., in 2016, we spent a lot of time in Birmingham with Tristan's sister Joss in her studio. Initially we took all of the ideas that we'd collated from analysing our favourite shirts and came up with our first iteration. We then wore the first design and found quite a lot of things we didn't like about it, so we went back and changed it. A lot of great design tweaks came from my gran. As someone who used to make her own clothes, she's very knowledgeable and called out issues with the initial design before we'd spotted them. We have a great family support network running all the way through the business.

We created several iterations before we were happy. But "happiness" with our product, for us, is very much a transient state, because every few months we reassess the design and make slight tweaks and changes. Our basic design philosophy is to produce a shirt that is a fixed size and style that someone could buy one of and then they'd know exactly what size they are, and there's a kind of ease of purchasing.

CRAFTING A CONSIDERATE BUSINESS

Sustainability is important to us as people. It underpins our whole practice. With an environmental law background, I have always had an interest in sustainability, the environment, renewable energy and topics surrounding them. I always knew if I started a business, I would make it as sustainable as possible. There are always going to be things that we can improve and make more sustainable, but I think having sustainability in mind is the right attitude to begin with. The landscape has changed quite a lot. Even in the few years we have been running the business, there are now far more brands that appear to be sustainable. We aim to create products with longevity and to develop a truly sustainable brand rather than taking advantage of the eco-friendly trend for marketing purposes.

The manufacture of all of our products is done in the UK. We would love to make everything in end-of-line UK fabrics, but as there is a limited supply, finding the right fabrics has been tricky. There are few UK-based fabric suppliers, and even fewer that make the fabric that we want. Because some of the end-of-line fabrics have been purchased by a warehouse from another warehouse or manufacturer, it can be difficult to trace the origins of a fabric. But that's something we're honest about, and are looking to address as much as possible. We are currently making enquiries to discover new UK-based companies we can work with. Everything has been a journey; we're still learning and we are always looking for new opportunities to become even more sustainable.

We will always aim to work to the highest possible standard and make sure we're offering something unique. Most of the design process happens with our manufacturers in the room; it's great to have everyone in one place to get input from everyone at the same time rather than having to have a disconnected back-and-forth. While we want to grow and increase in size, we still want to stay true to those values, so if we were to continue growing, there would be a point where we would consider putting in place a self-imposed limit on a level of production we're happy with. We have considered working with manufacturers in India, because there are a lot of really sustainable practices over there. It's incredibly difficult to decipher which is the most sustainable option, especially when you start to consider carbon footprint. As a result we're looking at working with a company that audits businesses and analyses their sustainability. There will always be people who will be critical of the extent of a business' sustainability, but the only thing you can do is learn as much as possible and do your best with it, you just have to say "We'll take that back to the drawing board and look at it again". I'm perfectly happy for people to challenge us and point out things to us that we haven't considered, whether that is in the design of the shirt or the practices we use.

> "Everything has been a journey; we're still learning and we are always looking for new opportunities to become more sustainable"

PROCESS OVERVIEW

01 The first step in the making process is the designing. Tristan and I draft an initial shirt design and work on it with our manufacturing team.

02 Tristan and I then visit end-of-line fabric suppliers and select our preferred materials. We closely check the quality and finish of the fabrics.

03 Once a pattern is drawn up for our shirt design, a member of the manufacturing team unrolls the chosen fabrics on the cutting table and carefully lays out the pattern pieces for the shirt. Each piece of the pattern corresponds to a panel of the shirt.

04 Once pinned in place, the pattern cutter then expertly cuts out all of the component parts of the shirt from the chosen fabric.

05 Another member of the team then sews the shirt panels together using a special heavy duty sewing machine to create extremely strong seams, perfect for our thicker fabric.

06 Finally, it is time for the finishing touches. The manufacturing team sew in the trimmings and tortoiseshell buttons.

"Most of the design process happens with our manufacturers in the room; it's great to have everyone in one place to get input from everyone"

01

02

04

03

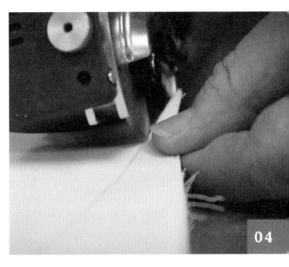

05

06

PUBLIC ENGAGEMENT

We mainly sell online, as well as through pop-ups in London and Bristol. Although there is a much wider market online, we're really keen to keep that face-to-face relationship-generating element of our sales. It gives us so much joy because we get the opportunity to meet our customers and get direct feedback from them about our products and what they like and dislike. I think people are more engaged when you can explain everything in person and show them all of the different products in the flesh, whereas online you are just another brand. You can tell your story well online but not anywhere near as well as face-to-face.

The best method of interacting with our customers online is through our Instagram feed. As Instagram is so visual, and offers the use of the Stories function, we can interact with people, and tell them what we're up to. It can be fun and light-hearted; I think it's more comfortable and engaging for readers that way.

KEEPING HONEST

I'd much prefer someone wear out all of their existing clothes before they come and buy some of our pieces, than throw all their existing stuff away and buy our shirts to be more "sustainable". Using solely new sustainable materials and leaving the less sustainable materials to become waste is not a solution. If it already exists and you like it, then you may as well use it. There are different schools of thought, but that's what we believe.

Most of our customers understand and appreciate the craft and the fact that our products are UK-made. What I think is really great is that we are starting to see people who previously weren't so interested, starting to care about the products they use and consume. High-profile court cases such as the air pollution case brought by Client Earth and campaigns for the reductions of plastics have made pollution a big topic on the public agenda. There is more in the news generally about sustainability and there is definitely an increased awareness of the lack of sustainability measures in the fashion industry.

To some extent we will always be in competition with larger brands, because if someone says "I need a new shirt", they have the option to come to us or they can go to any number of brands on the high street, or luxury fashion brands. Where I think the difference is, is that people who do know our story and ethos, are already interested in the same things. One of the challenges for us is to effectively spread the message about Grove & Co. and the things we stand for. We think it's always important to be humble and it's a privilege for someone to part with their hard-earned cash to buy one of our shirts over a well-known brand, so the onus is on us to tell people about what we can offer them. That's the reason that we use Instagram and try to get face-to-face as much as possible. It's so easy to convey your message when you can chat with someone for five minutes and explain why you do what you do.

THE FUTURE

Our main goal is to ensure we're making products that we love and our customers love. In terms of more complex goals, we would like to host more pop-ups and collection launch events which can give us greater exposure, and direct, invaluable contact with our buyers. Because we started this as a project which was focused on the product rather than the business purely as a money-making exercise, everything for us is product-driven. Constantly improving the product and bettering what we've done before will always be at the heart of what we do.

Every business can be more sustainable. What I believe we need to do is see how we can minimise our impact by reducing the environmental cost from raw materials, and once we've created that product, making it last for as long as possible to prolong its useful life before it's thrown away or recycled.

We try to use natural fibres wherever possible, so most of our heavy shirts are made from 100% cotton. Some of the woollen shirts we released previously had an element of manmade fibres in, and again it's always a trade-off, so if you buy a pure-wool shirt it will be biodegradable at the end of its life and have less impact throughout its lifecycle, but the flipside of that is it will wear out significantly faster. It's always a balancing act and it's something we consider at all stages of the manufacture, design, and sourcing.

> "Constantly improving the product and bettering what we've done before will always be at the heart of what we do"

At its simplest, I think the best way forward for the fashion industry is to produce high-quality items and move away from a model of fast consumption. It's not just a problem with the fashion industry, it's a wider societal consumption issue in the West. It is now typically how people live their lives; they consume and throw away. I think greater education and awareness is needed. The fashion industry could make people more aware of the many issues with the current linear fashion system, for example, one of the main environmental costs of clothing is the washing of it – you have a piece of clothing for years and each wash uses energy and water. The public need to be educated about the impact of their use of clothing as well as their purchasing of it. We have tried to do that in a simple way by including a wash care label telling you to wash the garment at low temperatures, and also by making overshirts which are designed to be worn over a T-shirt to minimise washing. Where possible, reducing consumption is always best.

MAYAMIKO

Paola Masperi
Malawi, Africa | mayamiko.com

CREATIVE BEGINNINGS

We have a team in Malawi of around fifteen to twenty people, working in production and training. We work with local community leaders to identify women that are particularly in need of our help and then we select a small number every six months to participate in tailoring and sewing training. Typically, at the end of the training, we offer a number of options to our graduates. One of which is to stay with us and learn how to produce fashion professionally within our workshop, and another is to take a grant from us to start their own business. Working in-house isn't suitable for everyone, so a lot of people jump at the opportunity to start their own business in their local community. We reconnect regularly and offer refresher training; we might get everyone back to learn a particular skill, for example last year we taught jewellery making using scrap offcut material. Some maintain a long-term relationship with Mayamiko and want to make sure they're doing well, and feel like they're connected and still belong.

> "We try to understand where there is a need and help that need, while collaborating with the community"

We have a number of initiatives that we do at a community level, for example, we work with a local organisation that works with out-of-school girls and orphans, and with them we deliver the sanitary pad initiative – using the offcuts from fashion production to create reusable pads that are donated to charity organisations across the world, including refugee camps, as well as to the local community. We work with a local charity which teaches about feminine hygiene and sexual health and then we provide the physical products. We also work with another local organisation that provides solar lighting for communities that don't have access to electricity. We try to understand where there is a need and help that need, while collaborating with the community – this is the overall concept of Mayamiko. We never wanted to be a charity that relies on donation or aid, we wanted to work to a sustainable model that could create long-term jobs, and bring long-term economic impact, as well as supporting people to be creative and share their traditions with the rest of the world.

MOTIVATION

Clothing connects people around the world; however different our clothing traditions may be, we all wear clothes, take pride in what we wear and feel that our clothes represent us and how we want to be perceived, so that was something that particularly stood out when we tried to identify where we could make an impact. Another important aspect of the Mayamiko ethos, is supporting traditional textile culture in Africa. Across Africa you'll see that in every village, there will be someone sewing beautiful pieces, and so our idea was to find a way to share them with the world while creating long-lasting opportunities, particularly for women. In Africa, traditional textile skills are dying out, as result of imported second hand clothing that a country like Malawi can't compete with, so local production has suffered. After speaking to many local women when we first set up Mayamiko, we felt that the tradition and culture of making clothing should be upheld and also shared with the rest of the world.

> "Clothing connects people around the world; however different our clothing traditions may be, we all wear clothes, take pride in what we wear and feel that our clothes represent us"

Currently there are lots of conversations surrounding cultural appropriation, as the brightly patterned prints that are commonly associated with African textiles, are actually of Dutch descent, so often questions are posed about whether they are really African. They are however, the textiles people would use locally and although Malawi doesn't have a particular tradition of specific textiles or techniques, there are other African countries that produce textiles specific to their traditions. From my point of view, it makes sense to utilise the textiles that are available locally and that the makers identify with. Through the vibrancy and bold patterns we bring to the world, we hope to really shine a light on the people that make the garments and their stories. It makes the clothes more valuable because you see the life that they have had before and you appreciate the process more.

Not only do we buy locally, we work locally – we employ local tailors and more than that, we co-create with our team. We work together to generate initial shapes and ideas, as well as considering finer details such as the print placement. Our designs generally incorporate very simple lines so that the bold prints can do the talking. From the moment we select and buy the textiles to when we finish the garment, it is a truly made-in-Africa product.

TREASURE IT

Think long and hard about what you buy to ensure you will love and treasure it for a long time. Take time to think a purchase through and as tempting as it might be, don't impulse buy!

We have been exploring working with refugee communities or post-conflict communities to use crafts as a way to make an income and also stay connected with their culture and traditions, which is often all they have left. While doing that research I realised that the mass-production, throwaway culture is being rejected in many areas of life, and there has been a swing back to something slow and mindful, with its own life and story, which is appreciated more than ever before.

Part of our founding strategy was to create a charity that could be sustainable and offer a creative outlet to local workers – I had no intention of creating a fashion label to purely make profit. We realised that for us to become competitive in terms of quality and production internationally, we needed to put a lot of effort into training and achieving the best possible sustainable standard. We thought that if we couldn't reach that point, then at least we will have trained a lot of people to become tailors so there would definitely be a positive outcome. The business funds the charity – I want Mayamiko to be a successful international label, but I don't want to do it for profit, I just want to continue the community work that we love so much. It is interwoven in the business model and making the charity sustainable and it's a crucial outlet for making money for the charity to keep it going and in turn, helping more people.

In terms of sustainability, people often ask whether we focus on the social impact or the impact on the environment, but I believe the two should not be disassociated – you can't be good to people if you're not being good to the planet at the same time; we constantly revise our model to improve this balance. There's always this conundrum: buy locally to lower carbon emissions and have a positive impact on the community, but potentially you won't know where those textiles came from originally, or import materials, organic certified cotton which ticks a lot of the boxes from the material point of view but still you have to fly it in. We decided to find a partner on the continent that creates organic cotton, so we're keeping it fairly local but also getting positive economic impact. We work with a company in Uganda that produces organic certified cotton and creates lots of jobs locally. We took the time to find the right partner, appreciating that buying locally has a positive community impact. Supplier chains are so complicated and intertwined, so it's very hard to get it all right. As long as you're transparent, people can make their own choices.

WASTE NOT, WANT NOT

We also design with fabric waste – offcuts are turned into something valuable, anything from the scrunchies and jewellery, to sanitary pads. We want to send the message that there is value in everything and to abandon the throwaway culture. Through creativity we're showing that offcuts can be valuable, rather than just waste to be thrown away. That's where co-creation becomes really exciting, you never know who will come up with the next idea, what can be done with those bits of fabric or how we could make the process more efficient – it's really collaborative in our team, everyone's always thinking!

It's common sense not to waste, now we talk about it as if it's such a wonderful thing that has just been discovered, but fifty years ago, I remember my granny, who used to sew as a hobby, would use leftover fabric to make little dresses for my doll. I think it's just about going back to things that make sense and not being wasteful, as a principle. There are always more ways you can improve, for example, the packaging we use for all of our products, (we don't use single use plastics, we have plastic containers that we put clothing in by the bulk and those plastic containers get recycled over and over again). When we ship something to a customer, we don't use plastic, we use paper and a compostable mailer that breaks down in six months in a compost bin. My attitude is that this is something to try out but could also be a disaster because if it's a hot day, the compost mailer might be affected and start breaking down. But if we don't try, we won't know and we want to continually improve. Becoming more sustainable in the future is an ongoing goal. I'm sure there are quicker ways to do things but sometimes the quicker way is quick for a reason. Often, it's at the expense of someone or something and because technology hasn't caught up with this level of recycling, you have to wait for things to be developed before you can put them in place.

> "... sometimes the quicker way is quick for a reason"

TOO GOOD TO BE TRUE

I would always distrust things that sound too good and too perfect because the supply chains and the fashion industry is so complex that if someone claims to have done it all, for a very low price, to me that sounds like a lie. Be curious and see where your values are and figure out where those values can match. For example, if empowering people is really important to you, find a brand that pays good wages and has a community project. Decide what matters to you as an individual and where you find those values in the choices that you make, otherwise it becomes too disheartening to address it all because no brand can really do it all.

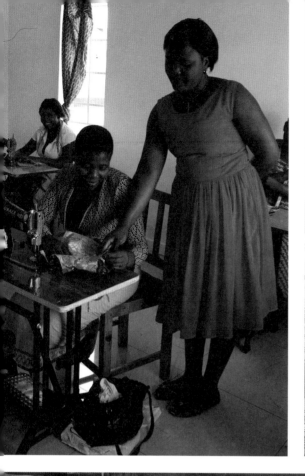
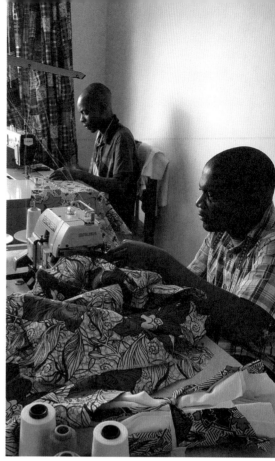

WORKSPACE

Our workspace is a large house with a huge garden around it. The multi-purpose space is used as a workshop as well as a showroom to display our products to visiting customers, and a classroom to teach trainees. As a live space, it's not a beautifully manicured showroom, but it is very welcoming, and highlights the importance of the process.

All of our furniture is made with local reclaimed wood – we have a fabric display made from reclaimed tree branches. The cutting table is in the showroom, and there is a desk for local managers to use. There's a separate room full of sewing machines – it's a great place for all of the tailors and seamstresses to communicate and work together during the making process. And there is also a classroom where all the training happens. It's all very open which gives the trainees chance to ask professionals for advice.

Upon entering, our customers are immersed in the beautiful fabrics and have the chance to experience first-hand how their garment is made. There's a big changing area where customers can try things on or we can take measurements. In the garden, we wash all the fabrics and dry them in the sun, and an array of lovely fabrics can often be seen swaying on the washing line. It's such a peaceful environment.

01

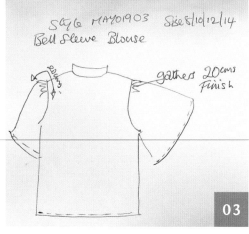

03

02

04

DRESSMAKING PROCESS OVERVIEW

01 The starting point of any Mayamiko garment is the fabric. Often as a team, we visit local markets to select and buy a range of different, colourfully printed fabrics.

02 After purchasing a large batch of fabric, and before starting work on creating a garment, we wash the fabrics and hang out to dry naturally in our outdoor space.

03 I then design a garment and develop a dressmaking pattern. During this process, I consider which fabrics we have purchased and how best to use the bold pattern with the shapes of the garment. I often keep the designs simple to give full attention to the fabric.

04 At the workshop, a member of the team pins the paper pattern pieces in place on the fabrics, with zero-waste cutting in mind. Any scrap offcut pieces are used later to create accessories such as jewellery, or sanitary pads for feminine hygiene charities as well as the local community.

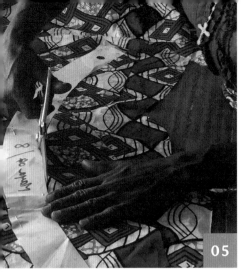

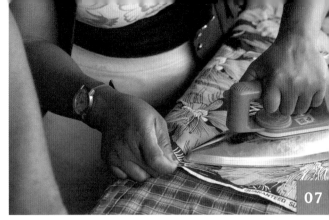

05

07

MAYAMIKO
DESIGNED

08

06

Meet my Maker

Discover my Story

09

05 Next, the individual pattern pieces that make up the garment are cut out of the fabric by hand, using sharp fabric scissors.

06 One of our seamstresses then sews the cut-out garment components together using a sewing machine. The pieces are first lined up at the coordinating seams and then sewn together to assemble the garment into one wearable piece.

07 Once the construction is complete, a Mayamiko label is sewn into the garment. To prepare the garment for retail, the entire garment is carefully pressed with a hot iron to remove any folds and small creases in the fabric.

08 Now that the garment is finished, we package it up using tissue paper and send to the customer wrapped inside a compostable mailing bag.

09 When the garment arrives with the customer, they can scan the unique QR code inside each piece to find out more about their purchase and connect to the team who made the garment.

THE DAY-TO-DAY

We start work at around 8.00 am, when the makers get into their overalls then go to their pigeon hole to collect the item they were previously working on. I currently spend less time at the workshop, because our aim was to set up the production unit to become independent so that it could produce for Mayamiko, but also for others.

During the working week, as well as making, many things will be happening. For example, parallel to the day-to-day dressmaking, new trainees will be taught, and marketing will be underway. We often try to work with local writers, photographers, and influencers to spread the word of Mayamiko. We also frequently arrange trips to the market to select fabrics. Everyone gets involved with everything, but when we choose fabrics everyone has an opinion!

I generally design the collection for the main range because for export we have to make sure certain standards are met and followed, such as shapes and sizes, to create a consistent brand identity. I've always had a sense of aesthetic and what I like, so cuts and lines are very simple but the colours and prints are bright. When choosing fabrics, I'll have a mood board and colour palette and we will all look at it and think about it together. For local customers, it's totally down to the team. The made-to-order pieces offer the team an opportunity to get really creative.

SOCIAL MEDIA: THE GREAT EQUALISER
Social media gives an equal voice to those who wouldn't otherwise have the opportunity to buy PR coverage that could give them a global reach. Instagram is really important for fashion and using the hashtags is great, whereas Facebook is more for checking that you're current and still going. The real engagement happens on Instagram.

THE FUTURE

Part of me wants Mayamiko to expand and grow so that it can make a bigger impact and help more people, but I'm torn, because that would mean selling more, and I need to consider whether it is better for the world if we sell better, and in a different way, rather than just selling more. We're exploring ways in which we can do things better and challenge the current business models. For me, a big success would be to integrate closed-loop systems into our workflow so that we can see the life of the garment as a continuum. I believe we are headed in the right direction with our latest collection, which contains QR codes that can be scanned to find out more about that individual garment. This allows customers to connect with the people that made the garment. In the future I hope this garment scanning will improve recycling, as it will be easy and quick to find out what a garment is made from and how best to reuse it.

Hopefully in the future, technology will be developed to increase sustainability and made-to-order designs. With more advanced technology such as 3D printing, I hope to see more garments being tailored to the consumer, with less likelihood of them being thrown away because they don't fit. I would also like to see more efficient making, so that we're not creating so much waste.

Success to me is about carrying on that journey and closing that loop, as well as connecting communities and people. I want Mayamiko to continue to evolve so that we can keep being as sustainable as possible. The business and charity supports a lot of people, so we have a responsibility to make sure we're doing the best for everyone involved.

VALUE YOUR VALUES

Really think about your values and what you're trying to achieve with your business. Then partner with people you've met with, researched, and also see it as a long-term partnership rather than just an experiment. Be strategic about where your values are and make sure your partners have the same values because when you want to change and approve things, they are more likely to listen and be creative with you.

MENDING

Mending refers to the repair of garments through the use of stitching, patching, or darning. A needle and thread can be used to add functional embroidery that is also beautiful. Mending inspiration spans cultures and continents including Japanese sashiko and boro; Indian kantha; European darning; and American patchwork quilting. Using simple stitches, these methods can reinforce worn textiles while illustrating another chapter in their story.

"... the reconnection is about considering our relationship to our garments and making intentional choices about what clothes we purchase, make, or tend"

Katrina Rodabaugh

KATRINA RODABAUGH

New York, USA | katrinarodabaugh.com

- -

CREATIVE BEGINNINGS

Although I hold a Bachelor's degree in Environmental Studies and a Master's degree in Creative Writing, and I've worked in the arts professionally since 2000, my creative training first started at the side of my mother's sewing machine. I am incredibly inspired by the history of craft. My mother, grandmother, and great-grandmother were all crafters. So, I appreciate this lineage in my own family and also from an historical arts and crafts viewpoint. I'm very interested in learning how cultures historically repaired, redesigned, or valued fibre and cloth. It's only very recently that we've discarded textiles at such a rapid pace. I love looking back across centuries and continents to see how people have tended to textiles with incredible innovation, craftsmanship, and care.

I have now been working in sustainability and arts organisations for two decades, but in 2013, I launched my slow fashion project, *Make Thrift Mend*, shortly after the Rana Plaza garment factory collapsed in Dhaka Bangladesh. It started as a one-year art project where I abstained from buying new clothing and focused on making simple garments, buying second-hand, and mending what I owned. *Make Thrift Mend* was intended to be a personal art project but I quickly realised it was more than a one-year experiment. I've been working with fibre arts since I was a child, so to some extent it was just my natural instinct to use those skills to repair and redesign my clothes.

I focus on repair, redesign, and reconnection in fashion. The repair work usually results in mending, darning, and patching. The redesign is typically patchwork, piecing, or working with dye plants that I've grown, foraged, or saved from my kitchen, and the reconnection is about considering our relationship to our garments and making intentional choices about what clothes we purchase, make, or tend. Within my creative practice, I enjoy the intersection of sustainable living, social practice in the arts, and my love of fibre arts. Once I realised these passions could come together in my wardrobe, there was no turning back.

MOTIVATION

I love being able to turn my background in the arts and textiles into very utilitarian solutions of mending, dyeing, and redesigning clothes. Sustainability is so important. As an artist and maker, I think it is my responsibility to consider sustainability in my work. I truly believe it is the future of all good design, and I think we have a responsibility to make work that is simultaneously beautiful, innovative, thoughtful, and ecocentric.

Mending, plant dyes, and sustainable style are at the centre of my creative work – keeping existing garments in rotation and out of landfill. On these topics, I teach workshops and retreats, publish articles and books, and share my techniques online and in person. But I also buy second-hand; prioritise eco-friendly, biodegradable materials in fibres and packaging; and consider the longevity of what I buy, use, or make. I grow my own dye plants, sustainably forage wild plants, and use my kitchen scraps for plant dyes. I compost, recycle, upcycle, and maintain a low-waste home and studio. I try to find uses for even the tiniest fibre scraps – and consider the hierarchy of functions with any materials. There are so many ways that my personal life and studio life intersect and I find that just strengthens my sustainable commitment – for example, my honeybees feed on the wild goldenrod flowers that I also forage for fibre dyes.

> "... we have a responsibility to make work that is simultaneously beautiful, innovative, thoughtful, and ecocentric"

Each day is somewhat different, depending on my deadlines. But my kids are typically in school from 9.00 am until 3.00 pm, so I try to keep my work within these hours. Of course, sometimes that's not possible with teaching retreats, hosting events, or meeting big deadlines, but I try to put my work away from the time my kids are home from school until they're asleep at night. I love having focused time with them and they ground me in a very meaningful way – they're truly my biggest motivation.

MAKING SPACES

I live in an 1820s farmhouse in the Hudson Valley of Upstate, New York. We moved to this house in 2015 and have steadily been DIY renovating ever since. I have three workspaces but two are seasonal. The carriage barn has been renovated into my working and teaching space, but it's only available May to November because of our harsh winters. We've also created a natural dye lab in the back of our garage but it's seasonal too. Then I have a bedroom upstairs in our farmhouse that I use year-round. Plus, the gardens also function as my workspaces in the summer months.

My mending tools are simple: thread, needles, scissors, thimbles, fabric pencil, and a ruler. I love that mending tools are portable, affordable, and basic sewing tools that many folks might already own.

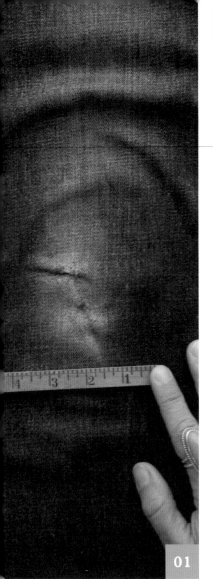

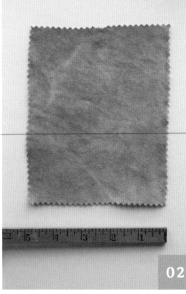

02

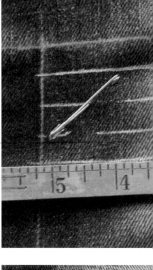

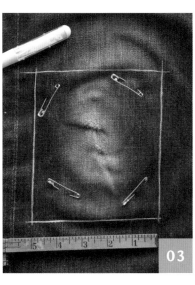

01

03

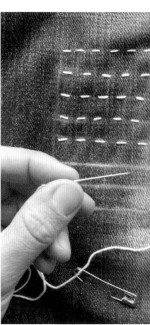

MENDING PROCESS OVERVIEW

01 First, I place the garment flat on a work surface and measure the distressed area I want to repair. I add an inch to the measurements on all sides, to work out the correct size for the patch.

02 For long-lasting repairs, I use the same weight and fibre for patch and thread as the garment. I cut the patch to size using pinking shears. Delicate fabrics, such as linen and silk, should have finished patch edges on all sides.

03 Next, I slide the patch underneath the distressed materials, and pin through to the top of garment with safety pins. I then trace the edges of the patch with a fabric pencil to provide a stitching guide.

04 I draw several parallel, horizontal lines with a fabric pencil on the exterior of the garment. These lines will help make straight lines of stitches when mending. Stitches aren't meant to be perfect, but these guides keep the work tidy.

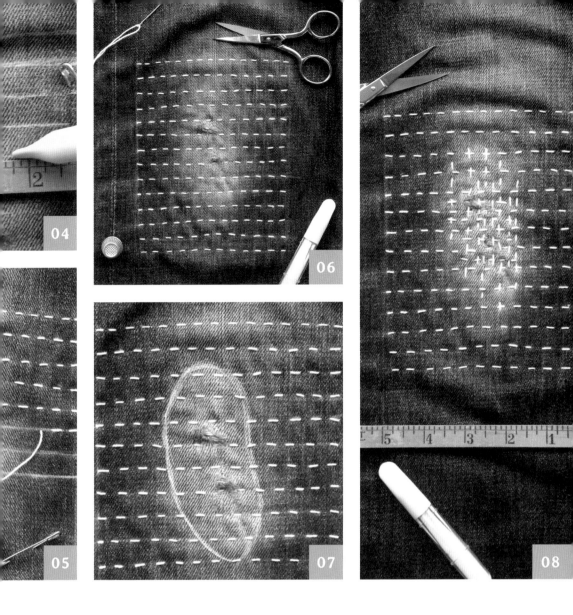

05 I then thread the sewing needle and begin stitching from the underside of the patch, keeping the knotted end of the thread inside the garment. I start running wide stitches across each horizontal guide line.

06 Next, I continue to stitch until I have completely covered the area to be repaired with lines of running stitch. If the fabric pencil guide lines fade, I simply stop and sketch them again.

07 Next, I add vertical stitches. I outline the distressed or damaged area of the garment and concentrate the vertical stitches here. The shape can be abstract and organic or more regimented.

08 I draw vertical lines down the outlined shape using a fabric pencil and repeat the running stitches as before until all edges of the holes are secured and the damaged area is sufficiently repaired.

HOLDING TOGETHER

My work centres around teaching and sharing knowledge regarding sustainable fashion. I teach workshops across the United States and I host annual retreats in my converted barn. I publish articles and tutorials through blogs, magazines, and books, and I offer a limited selection of crafting kits, plant-dyed textiles, and subscription kits online. I also collaborate with artists, designers, and sustainable fashion brands from time-to-time.

After many years of living between New York City and the San Francisco Bay Area, I now live in a very small town in Upstate New York. The Internet makes my work possible from this remote, rural location. I'm very grateful for social media, digital newsletters, and online shops.

I worked in arts galleries, theatres, and urban arts spaces for sixteen years and I received incredibly valuable information about craftsmanship, voice, vision, and authenticity in the arts. This is imperative, of course. But I think many artists still lack business training. We aren't really taught about business models, financial planning, how to scale, or how to create long-term financial stability. I think this is the biggest threat to small, creative businesses and working artists – how to plan for growth, create sustainable financial systems, and secure the support we need to do this work for decades. Of course, it's possible to succeed. But it takes a tremendous amount of drive, organisation, and resourcefulness, as well as risk navigation. I worry that so many artists are exhausted from being DIY entrepreneurs that they won't have the stamina to keep making creative work. Hopefully, we all find the resources we need to grow and thrive.

There is however, a huge sense of community among crafters. I see this mostly in the workshops and retreats I teach and host. Even if there wasn't a sense of familiarity when the workshop starts, it's palpable by the end, especially at a multi-day retreat. But I also experience community online and through social media. Hopefully, the community will continue to expand to support the various needs of people of all lifestyles, professions, aesthetics, classes, races, genders, orientations, cultures, and geographies. I really hope slow fashion can be a movement that supports all people.

RECONNECT WITH THE PLANET

Get close to the earth physically. Take hikes, go camping, birdwatch, grow food and herbs, and wander through your city parks identifying plants. I think the more we can repair our disconnection to the natural world, the better. In any environment there's an opportunity to connect deeper with nature – follow the moon phases from your skyscraper or grow more food from your backyard. We are dependent on this planet for our survival. We need to connect with that basic need. And then, of course, research and read everything you can find about how to make your work more sustainable.

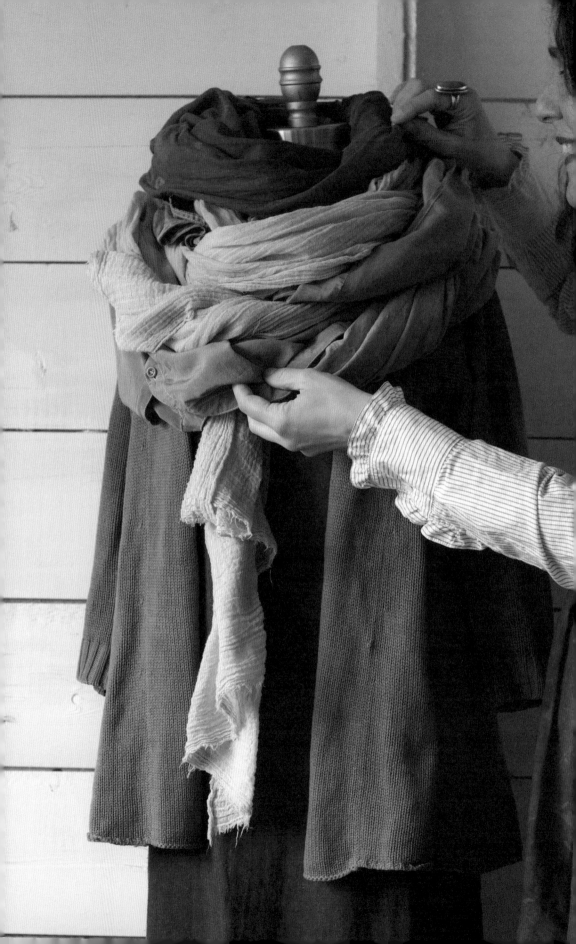

STYLE TRANSCENDS TREND

I definitely do not try to keep on trend. Actually, I often try to keep away from trends as much as possible. When I started *Make Thrift Mend* in 2013, it became apparent that trends were a huge part of the problem with a disposable fashion mindset. When I buy, make, or design clothing I try to ask myself three questions – Do I love this? Do I need this? Can I wear this for a minimum of five to ten years? If I can't answer "yes" to all three questions, it's not the right garment for me.

I think style is really about tuning into our inner aesthetic, intuition, self-awareness, and self-acceptance. Style transcends trends, or proceeds them, instead of chasing them. I think the closer we get to our personal style, the farther we can get away from shifting trends. That said, of course, there is also a zeitgeist. There is a collective aesthetic resulting from current interests, insights, politics, and economics and I'm not immune to the zeitgeist, but I don't intentionally chase trends.

"With basic awareness, we can create really radical shifts"

Competing with big brands is so hard for so many small businesses and independent artists, especially when trying to use fair labour and eco-friendly materials which often cost much more than conventional materials. There's no way I can compete with huge manufacturers in terms of labour costs, materials, or shipping fees, so, I try not to compete at all. I try to focus on offering limited-edition goods with handcrafted details that add value and meaning – such as textiles dyed with plants from my garden. I also try to focus on sharing knowledge so folks can learn to mend, dye, or style a sustainable wardrobe and then adapt that information into their lives. I think the more we can share information about material costs, labour-intensive handwork, and the challenges of making sustainable garments and goods, the more we can start to shift the consumer expectations and understanding of value.

MINDFUL SHOPPING

Slow down your consumption and consider second-hand when possible, prioritise eco-friendly materials, insist on fair labour, practice handmade skills, or just repair what you already own. It's amazing what can happen when we just slow down. I think mindfulness is one of the biggest opportunities for impact. With basic awareness, we can create really radical shifts.

THE FUTURE

I love my work. I love being able to combine my training in sustainability, my professional experience in the arts, and my passion for fibre arts, and then share this work publicly. My plans are to keep getting clearer on my priorities as an artist and a small sustainable business – How can I refine my vision to better align with my core values while still creating opportunities for growth? But I also really love publishing and the combined opportunity to share handcrafts, style photoshoots, and write about sustainable fashion. I'd love to be able to host more events and retreats in my space – to create a physical venue for people to gather to create innovative solutions. But, mostly, I want to support more people in their journeys with slow fashion.

"I want to support more people in their journeys with slow fashion"

I think circular fashion provides a huge opportunity for future evolution and improvement across the retail sector. Fair labour also needs to become an absolute guarantee. I'm inspired by small companies maintaining a commitment to eco-friendly materials, living wages, zero or low-waste, and growing at a manageable rate. For big companies, I'm most inspired by the few brands trying to create circular systems by taking responsibility for their clothes post-consumer – repairing, redesigning, and even re-weaving or felting fibres from cast-off clothes, that's so exciting.

FELT MAKING

Raw wool or other natural fibres are torn into tufts and fused together using hot, soapy water and friction. Layers of the fibres are compressed together through the friction and heat to create a sheet of felt. Once the felt has dried it can be dyed, printed, and used to craft a multitude of garments, accessories, or homewares.

- -

"I am incredibly proud of our Uruguayan Merino wool as it's produced locally, certified, and traceable – it's the perfect material!"

Alice Otegui, Calmo

CALMO

Alice Otegui
Uruguay | calmoslow.com

CREATIVE BEGINNINGS

I've known since I was little that I wanted to be a fashion designer because I have always had a love for textiles. As I grew up I started developing a great interest in the creative processes involved in building a universe around a product, and the infinite possibilities of making a positive impact with my work. Calmo started as a womenswear and textile art brand, but now offers a much wider range of products, including homewares. All products are handmade by local artisans in Uruguay. Every piece is one of a kind, crafted from natural materials, using sustainable processes, including hand felting and natural printing. I adore textile experimentation and traditional hand crafts, so I always envisioned that Calmo could expand further to become even more sustainable and create a range of different products, including other accessories, such as bags and jewellery, as well as ceramics, furniture and even cosmetics. I realised though that Calmo couldn't do it all just yet, and we needed to focus on one step at a time.

"It started very small, but grew organically"

In 2016 I applied for an incubator scheme in Uruguay called Socialab that supports entrepreneurs and social enterprises. I went to them with just the samples I had made and an idea of creating sustainable fashion using natural dyes and prints. I explained that I wanted to work with talented local artisans to supply them with an outlet for their work and a stable income. I wanted to create a beneficial social impact by providing employment to local people, consider the wider environment through the use of natural materials, and promote traditional crafts to bring respect back to craft and keep local traditions alive.

In January 2017, I launched Calmo. My collection was really small, with just a few styles. Nonetheless, as January is the peak of the summer season in Uruguay, I knew I needed to have some pieces ready for tourists visiting the area. The response was beautiful. It started very small, but grew organically.

MOTIVATION

Calmo's ethos of "slow and conscious" refers to the fact that we create products that are sustainable and contribute to slow fashion. I love hand crafts and their unique aesthetic. I adore items that are made with more profoundness, and not just to follow trends. In 2010, while studying, I participated in a student exchange at Parsons School of Design and that's when I discovered what sustainability was really about. It's about both social and environmental consciousness, all the way through the production process and throughout the lifespan of a product. This planted the seed of what would become a sustainable slow fashion brand. In February 2016 I learned natural dyeing and printing methods from a local artisan and fell in love with them. I saw great potential in it and thought I had to do something with these beautiful techniques! It inspired me to make products that would be aesthetically pleasing and tell a wonderful story, while also being competitive and exportable. I wanted to show a different side to Uruguayan design and crafts, and highlight our special textiles. That is the general concept of the Calmo brand, to bring back traditional crafts with a modern twist.

I am incredibly proud of our Uruguayan Merino wool as it's produced locally, certified, and fully traceable – it's the perfect material! I want it to be the star feature of our products. Our artisans create handmade felt, a typical Uruguayan material that has been passed down by generations of artisans, and that is slowly being forgotten. Often, when I explain to customers that we make handmade felt jackets, the common assumption is that they will be hard and itchy, but it is quite the opposite. The soft, workable quality of our Merino wool means that it can be used in so many different ways. For example, soon we will also be developing a knitted and woven collection. Apart from Merino wool, we also use other natural fibres, such as silk, linen, and cotton. We don't have local production of such textiles in Uruguay, therefore they have to be imported. I understand that it's not ideal due to the carbon footprint associated with imports, however we try to diminish our environmental impact in all other aspects of the production process.

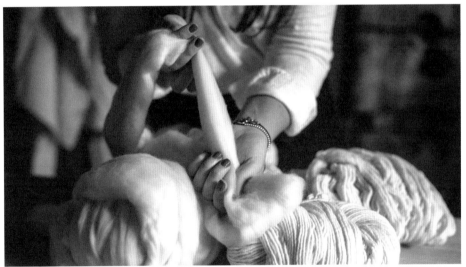

It is impossible to be 100% sustainable, especially at the beginning, so I have adopted the motto of "one step at a time". My goal is to use only outsourced materials that are certified and/or organic. We do our best to acquire materials from trustworthy sources, and treat them as responsibly as possible. I practice the mindset of "once I have it in my hands, I will do the best I can with it". I think sustainability is all about being resourceful and respectful. If you try to do everything from the beginning, you risk getting overwhelmed and just throwing in the towel. And if you push your workers and consumers to consider all the things that must be done to become more sustainable, it can scare and overwhelm them too. I don't see radicalism as a good path.

My core motivation in life is to inspire through my work; to inspire others to follow their passion, but also to teach that there's value in people and nature. That message translates to the Calmo brand and makes social and environmental impact an important factor. Through Calmo I hope to bring awareness to the need to take better care of ourselves, others, and the environment in which we live.

SLOW AND CONSCIOUS

At Calmo we follow the concept of slow production. The idea of "slow fashion" is a more sustainable approach than "fast fashion" as the time spent making the product is not set by the market, but by the processes and the people involved. There is an increased respect for nature, as the source of the materials, and respect for people because they can take their time in a healthy way to make a product. That respect is evident in the results. You can tell when something is made with time.

Increasing sustainability is not just about what you can do, it's also about bringing awareness, to show others what they can do. We can't have change if we don't know how or why. When we use our website or Instagram account to communicate, we try to explain what "sustainable" means to us. Our clothing tags also tell the customer who made them, what they are made from, and how to take care of a garment. Caring for your clothes is really important as it can increase the usability and prolong its life.

All of the materials we use are natural, in order to create a more biodegradable product. We use natural dyes because botanical dyeing is a beautiful environmentally friendly craft to preserve. We do use a tiny percentage of artificially dyed materials, such as black fabric, which I believe adds a lot to the overall aesthetic of my pieces. Although I want to work as sustainably as possible, I don't want to sacrifice the quality and aesthetic of my products. I want to create attractive saleable garments because I also need to consider economical sustainability. If products aren't desirable then the business won't work and you won't be able to do any of the other good, sustainable aspects of the business.

Where possible I only use offcut materials rather than having anything less sustainable made specifically for our products. I try to design in order to avoid waste because I am aware that the textile industry is responsible for producing tonnes of waste and contributing to already overflowing landfill sites. Most of the patterns we use feature geometrical cuts and are zero-waste designs; I love designing in that way as it is both sustainable and creatively challenging.

"You can tell when something is made with time"

THE COMPLEXITIES OF SUSTAINABILITY

Calmo's philosophy is to leave as little negative impact on the planet as possible, and to put the needs of the worker first. In my opinion, there is no sense in making an organic T-shirt if it's made in a sweatshop. To me, after the worker, the next most important aspect to consider is the environment: following the circular economy model to create biodegradable products, reducing our carbon footprint as much as possible, and ensuring a good standard of animal welfare.

Sustainability is a complex word, because it may be that something that is sustainable for some, is not sustainable for others. The important thing is that we are all aiming towards the same objective, and we just need to see what unites us instead of what sets us apart. There are many points of view and we need to be flexible and tolerant. For example, wool is one of the most honest raw materials, but many people believe that it's not very sustainable. I know that our wool is sourced from a company that has very high standards in terms of animal welfare, but I know that in other parts of the world, that isn't always the case. We simply cannot make generalisations. Instead of criticism, we need to be more positive to create a beneficial environment in which we can support each other and grow from our differences. There are many different approaches and degrees of sustainability.

When we first started, our tags contained information about the terrible impact of the fast fashion industry, but I then realised that it was quite a negative message to be hanging from our products. It is important for people to know what's happening, but it was also a bit overwhelming. I realised that the way forward is not through negativity, and shock tactics, but instead it is better to connect the buyer with their item on a positive level. By simply writing the name of the artisan who crafted each item on its tag, we can tell our customers the story behind each scarf or tunic, and encourage them to read between the lines and consider how, where, and by whom their clothes were made. Part of the process is learning. Instead of saying what you cannot do, it's about how we can do things better. Staying positive, not bringing a negative atmosphere to the issue keeps sustainability from becoming stressful and overwhelming.

THE WHOLE PACKAGE

Calmo is detail-centred; I consider every detail, down to the handwritten tag, the packaging, and of course, the garment itself. Every piece is one of a kind. And I think that through that kind of attention to detail, we can show that there's passion behind it, and that Calmo is much more than just a business.

Our packaging is just as important to us as what comes inside it. I want to create a whole brand experience, and believe that how you receive a product is just as important as the item itself. People really appreciate our packaging. Most items come in cotton bags, and the silk scarves come in locally made eucalyptus wood boxes, with a little branch of eucalyptus nestled inside the box. The garment tags are made from textiles or recycled paper. We always try to take the most sustainable option, while staying true to our overall aesthetic.

> "I believe that globally we're going back to craftsmanship, and to our natural origins"

There seems to have been an increased appreciation of crafts in recent years. Sustainability and hand-making have become worldwide and hopefully long-term trends. I believe that globally we're going back to craftsmanship, and to our natural origins, as a reaction to the speed of consumerism and pollution. I hope that it will not become just another trend, but be accepted as the only way to work. Because as they say, "there's no Planet B".

THE DAY-TO-DAY

At the beginning, I worked with just a few different artisans – seamstresses, felt makers, and dyers, and the team grew from there. It evolved and we now work with more than ten artisans, including seamstresses, a printmaker who screen prints our labels, and a carpenter who makes our boxes by hand. Most importantly, our artisans' work is formalised and flexible, so they can work from their homes and adapt their routine to suit their needs and the needs of their families.

We want to support our artisans with a fair and stable income in exchange for their work. But we also want to inspire them to be creative in the work they do alongside us. We like them to expand their own businesses and continue learning while they do so, as we have very high quality standards which require the best techniques and finishes. We want them to be able to make a living from their crafts, while truly enjoying what they do.

As Creative Director, it can be difficult to wear all the hats in the company, and sometimes the ideas are more romantic than the reality. As the brand grows and I become more involved in the business side of the company, time for creativity shrinks. But I really enjoy creative moments, such as when the artisans give me the rolls of botanically printed fabric to open and reveal the amazing patterns – it's very fulfilling.

As entrepreneurs, we also need to make time for our well-being. Starting your own business is challenging on so many levels, and can become anxiety inducing. I would call this the "sustainability of the founder". If we don't take good care of ourselves too, our businesses and their beautiful potential won't develop. In my case, I try to rest well, meditate every morning, eat healthily, and spend quality time with family and friends. I also always set aside some time to indulge in a good book and stay in touch with nature.

MAKE TIME FOR CREATIVITY

Schedule time for creative moments because otherwise there is an email to answer, or something else that needs to be done that will fill up your time.

WORKSPACES

I work at my mother's house. She paints with oil on canvas and she has an amazing studio filled with easels, which I have slowly started to invade. It's a very inspiring environment. Ever since I was young, my family home has been filled with art books and the inspiring aroma of oil paint.

My studio space is somewhere between the oils and the painted canvas, where I have a big wooden table and my dressmaking mannequin. Inside the studio you'll see lots of scissors, pencils, and pens and of course, fabric. When I design, I work directly on to the mannequin with fabric. I have different design processes, but I mostly enjoy being experimental and just cutting and seeing what happens. First, I craft with muslin, and then I move on to the final printed material, to avoid wasting any of the precious botanically printed fabric. I also draw and have lots of sketchbooks.

The Calmo team of artisans use a variety of tools. First, the plants; the source of the natural dye, and the raw materials for the natural dyes and prints. Then they need a huge table to print or create the felt on. When producing the botanical prints, large pots are required to boil the fabric in order to set the prints in place. All of these tools are needed in the artisans' homes to allow for flexible working.

BE AUTHENTIC

Never forget your origins. It's very important to stay local because that's how you make a product that resonates with you and your audience, and that has a lovely story behind it. You can create something very personal and authentic.

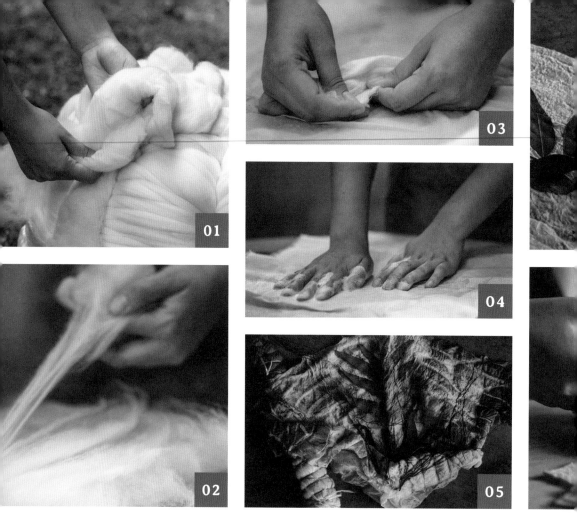

FELTED JACKET PROCESS OVERVIEW

01 First I source our beautiful certified RWS Uruguayan Merino wool from local farms. I prefer to use 18 micron fibres, as this fineness combines the softness we need for a perfect touch, with a reasonable fibre length to avoid pilling as much as possible.

02 The wool is made into felt by our artisans. Depending on the final product and drape I need, I ask them to make the felt with a specific thickness. The size of the felted piece also varies, in order to avoid textile waste. They then cover a table with bubble wrap and lay the raw combed wool fibres on top. Taken from the wool top, the wool is torn into tufts and overlapped and layered in various directions.

03 For the Pupa Jacket, I use a nuno felt, which is a type of felt that contains a mix of both Merino wool and silk fibres. The silk gives the felt an incredible extra texture, and a lovely subtle shine. A layer of silk fibres is added on top of the wool tufts.

04 Once assembled, the artisan moistens the felt with hot, soapy water, and covers with cotton muslin. The artisan then gently rubs and applies pressure to the muslin in order to create friction and heat. During this process the fibres compress and felt together. The entire felting process can take about three hours.

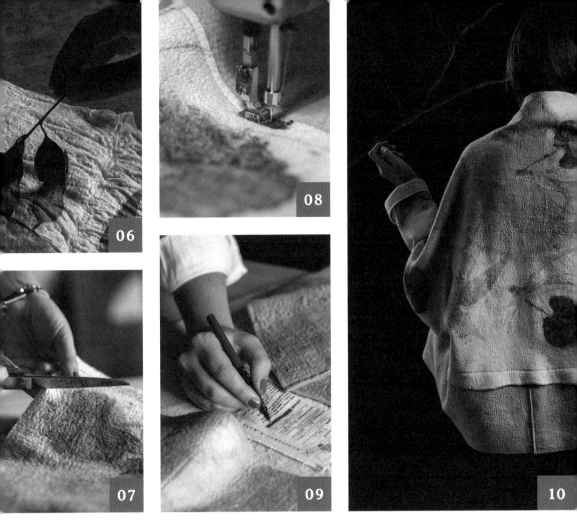

05 The nuno felt is ready to be eco-printed. An artisan layers local leaves, flowers, and other natural elements onto the felt and folds and ties the felt together to contain the leaves while it boils. After boiling, the bundles are left to dry in the sun for three days.

06 Once dry, the artisan opens the bundle to reveal the beautiful patterns within. All natural elements are removed and the felt is washed to remove any excess dye. Once dry, the artisan patiently irons the felt using a high temperature and steam. This allows the felt to stretch and reach the required size, while straightening it out to make it easier to work with.

07 Before cutting the fabric at my studio, I consider how I will make the most of each printed textile. Like the Pupa Jacket, most of our styles are born from geometrical shapes, so there is no need for traditional paper patterns. With just a guide, I can decide exactly how I will cut the felt. I just need to mark it with a mechanical pencil and a ruler first.

08 Once the jacket has been cut out, I pass the pieces on to our seamstresses, who stitch it together with an industrial sewing machine.

09 and 10 Once the jacket is finished, I write on the label the names of the artisans who worked on it, and the materials used.

CHALLENGES

The biggest threat to running a sustainable business in Latin America is the cost. Uruguay is a country where the cost of living and the cost of labour is really high. We pay our artisans fairly, but materials and processes are also costly, and taxes are always a challenge for any new business. Materials such as silk need to be imported and subsequently cost much more than local materials, so we are often limited by what we can afford and source.

Sustainable labels cannot be cheaper than fast fashion brands, because the methods are artisanal and involve slow processes and time-honoured skills, and are therefore more costly. Through our unique collections, we aim to compete on added value, originality and design, not with price. We as consumers need to buy less, and better. Take a T-shirt for instance: rather than purchasing five inexpensive disposable ones, we can choose to buy one T-shirt made under fair conditions, using sustainable materials that will last. It's all about how you tell the story of the product – if you don't tell your story effectively, people won't know why you are different, why your process is better, and they just won't understand why you're more expensive. It's about the message and the real impact you can have with your company.

Mass-market products are difficult to compete with, but it makes you very aware of the need to sell in order to survive. You can also learn from larger companies because they are experts in selling and tapping into what the consumer wants. They are mainly focused on the business side of fashion, something I, as a passionate creative, sometimes lack. I learn from them to be a little more business-oriented in order to survive in the world of business.

For small emerging brands like Calmo, social media is how you connect to the rest of the world. We cannot afford big publicity strategies, or fashion shows. Social media is perfect for us because it's the only way we can get our products to be seen by people everywhere. I think that the tricky part is to stay true to the brand values. For instance, as a brand I don't make huge end-of-season sales because the product is seasonless, so I don't want sales or other marketing strategies that are not in line with my brand. I need to have followers, but I don't want them at any cost. Social media has to be used in a responsible way, to stay transparent and honest.

A BEAUTIFUL FUTURE

In the near future I plan to open an online shop and build Calmo's presence abroad to spread the message of sustainability. My ultimate goal, is to have full traceability on all products, and as much transparency as possible. Moreover, I see Calmo as a brand of collaborations: I think that would be a very effective business model and a very beautiful experience. My dream is to collaborate with businesses across the world, to make a range of different products.

Sustainability is a process, and each day I try to make more responsible decisions, but it is impossible to be entirely sustainable. There's a beauty in the challenge of sustainability. When you take a local material and traditional technique and use it to address a social problem, you create something completely unique, with a history of its own. I see myself building projects in this way, always concentrating on sustainability as I believe it is the only way forward. I aim to bring profoundness back to design, taking into consideration three aspects: beauty, (we want to make attractive and inspiring products), a social aspect, and an environmental aspect. And when you combine those elements, you have a product that has a story that is powerful, and totally one of a kind.

I believe the fashion industry needs to take action towards sustainability one step at a time. When I was feeling overwhelmed by all the little things I wasn't doing instead of focusing on what I was doing, it really helped me to read *The Responsible Company* by the founder of Patagonia, Yvon Chouinard. I felt inspired and enlightened because it demonstrates this concept in an excellent way, explaining that you should follow these steps: take one step at a time, know where you have to be better and aim for it, and share what you learn. That philosophy is more realistic and forgiving, because trying to fix everything at once becomes overwhelming, and unsustainable long term. Be honest in terms of what you can do and what you cannot do. If you can do more, do more. Any little change is good.

KNITTING

Knitting is the method in which yarn is manipulated with the use of large needles to create a variety of different garments. The knitting process creates fabric consisting of rows of multiple intertwining loops of yarn, called stitches, in a line or tube. Knitting patterns can be followed to create specific garments. Knitting may be done by hand or by using a machine.

- -

"Due to the versatility of knitting, knitwear can be easily adapted to appeal to today's fashionable market audience"

Karen Sissal Kjartansdóttir Kristiansen, Shisa Brand

SHISA BRAND

Karen Sissal Kjartansdóttir Kristiansen
Tórshavn, Faroe Islands | shisabrand.com

- -

CREATIVE BEGINNINGS

Although I've always been both creative and good with my hands, I never expected that I would pursue a career as a designer. My mind was set on getting a degree in business or politics, so I went on to study a Master's degree in business and marketing. Since graduating in 2000 I worked as a teacher at a business school and as a brand consultant at an advertising agency on the Faroe Islands. Although I really loved working at the advertising agency, with great co-workers and clients, I just decided to quit on a random Monday morning. No drama and no specific plans, other than if I were to give this Shisa Brand a try, it had to be now.

With a heartfelt love for knitting and protecting the environment, my designs are a clash of deep-rooted Faroese culture and modern innovation. The Faroese have a long history of handknitting, and it is very common for girls to learn how to handknit at an early age, and I was no exception. Alongside the Faroese influences, I am also hugely inspired by Japanese aesthetics. It is the simplicity, clean lines, attention to detail, and the less-is-more feeling you get when you observe the Japanese style that I find most captivating.

"With a heartfelt love for knitting and protecting the environment, my designs are a clash of deep-rooted Faroese culture and modern innovation"

MOTIVATION

I love to knit; it is a beautiful craft and when you master knitting you can create many versatile patterns as well as a variety of different garments. Traditionally knitting is what the Faroese people have always done, and knitwear was the first product the Faroese exported. Living off the ocean and land, the Faroese make use of the plentiful fish from the sea for sustenance, and sheep wool for warmth – knitted wool sweaters kept fisherman warm on their fishing expeditions. The yarn used is mainly from free-range Faroese sheep. Locally hand-knitted sweaters, made with local yarn, rank highly on the sustainable charter. Even as exports they are still considered sustainable. Due to the versatility of knitting, knitwear can also be easily adapted to appeal to today's fashionable audience.

Making use of local materials is a very sustainable and connected way of living. Personally, I am of the belief that the story and the quality of the knitted sweater is better when knitted by hand. Of course, there are great machine-knitted sweaters, but there is something special about a garment that has been ten days in the making rather than an afternoon's work. And that is the story I like to tell. Who made it, where the wool came from, and what inspired the design.

> "As followers of fashion, we need to consider what kind of footprint our vanity leaves; environmentally, socially, and culturally"

Shisa Brand has been sustainably conscious from the very beginning, but has become even more ecologically aware with the growth of the brand. As I wish for Shisa Brand to grow bigger, I need to be conscious of what cost that has to the environment. As followers of fashion, we need to consider what kind of footprint our vanity leaves; environmentally, socially, and culturally. And we need to decide if we will be part of the fast fashion movement or choose slow fashion, which I believe is the origin of all fashion.

I feel that consumers have become more aware of the sustainable variable, of course not all, but the number of conscious consumers is definitely growing, and fast! With the increasing awareness of the environmental situation that we are in, more designers have taken sustainable fashion to be their focus and many are extremely talented. This has made it possible to talk about sustainable fashion and not only sustainable clothing. This new wave of sustainable fashion inspires both consumers and new designers, and pushes the industry to evolve.

WORKSPACE

As a knitter, all I really need are some knitting needles and some yarn and I am good to go – and therefore I can work almost anywhere I like, be it a café, visiting friends, or in my shop. I also make wallets and bags, so I also occasionally require my cutting mat and industrial sewing machine. I mostly work from home, where I can really focus, and I have all my knitting needles, yarn, patterns, and notebooks nearby – but it is also where my favourite knitting chair is located: a chair I inherited from my grandmother, who was also a great knitter.

Working from your own home has its pros and cons. It is a blessing to be surrounded by all these lovely materials that get my creativity working, but work and free time tend to merge, and as work often comes with deadlines and so many new ideas, it can be very difficult to take time off. Luckily, I enjoy creating, so although I might work most waking hours, it doesn't feel like it.

KNITTED JUMPER PROCESS OVERVIEW

01 To begin, I make a sketch of the design, sometimes very detailed, sometimes only a quick drawing on my phone. After the initial thought or idea, the yarn and colours inspire and inform the pattern. In this case, it was this exact yarn and colours that dictated the design.

02 Then I knit. Sometimes the pattern works perfectly, but often I will have to make a few alterations after having made the first sweater, to ensure subsequent garments are more refined.

03 This particular design is more difficult to knit, as the two colours of yarn mean that I have to keep a firm eye on the pattern itself. The single colour version is much quicker and easy to knit without full concentration on the pattern.

04 When the sweater is finished, knitted and sewn together, it has to be dampened down and pressed with a hot iron. This is one of my favourite moments as it really shows how the final piece will look.

05 The final step, before the sweater is ready for use, is to sew the Shisa Brand label onto the garment.

06 The finished sweater, ready to be sold, worn and loved.

> "Living off the ocean and land, the Faroese make use of the plentiful fish from the sea for sustenance, and sheep wool for warmth – knitted wool sweaters kept fisherman warm on their fishing expeditions"

01

02

03

04

05

06

CRAFTING A LIVING

Hand crafting unique knitted sweaters and making a living is very difficult, and it definitely does not make a luxurious living. As I have a lot of experience in advertising and tourism, I do have different consultant jobs in these areas which helps to support me, but my ultimate goal is to be able to afford to work full time at Shisa Brand, and I am getting closer and closer to achieving that.

Mostly I sell to the Faroese on the Faroe Islands, but in August 2018 I opened a shop with designer and brand Steinum in Tórshavn. This has changed my situation somewhat. First of all, I am working in the shop half of its open hours, but it has also made it easier for me to get in direct contact with my customers. With the shop, I have been even more conscious of spreading the word about Shisa Brand, mainly online via Instagram. But we also focus on spreading the word about the shop – Ullvøruhúsið – as it is a great way to attract tourists who come to the shop to buy gifts to take back to their home countries, becoming great ambassadors for our shop and brands. Meeting people face-to-face and talking about the product – the design and thoughts behind it, as well as the wool, and origin of knitting on the Faroe Islands – is the best way to connect with the customer and inspire them to care for the garment. Appreciating and caring for a garment will help it to live so much longer, and in that situation everyone wins – the environment and customer, as well as the story of Shisa Brand and the Faroe Islands.

SUSTAINABLE GROWTH

Making handmade garments in one of the most expensive countries in the world makes it very difficult to compete with big international brands that often have their garments produced in lower cost countries. Therefore, the importance lies in telling the story, about the Faroe Islands, the traditions and the Faroese wool and its exclusivity.

The future of Shisa Brand poses a bit of a dilemma between earning money and sticking to my principles and core idea. It is tempting to outsource the production to other countries, where my sweaters can be knitted cheaper and in greater quantities, but then I would turn away from the essence of Shisa Brand, being a knitwear brand that celebrates the knitting traditions of the Faroe Islands and honouring the Faroese wool. In the future, I do expect to have to create a machine-knitted line, because I need my volume to increase in order to make a living, and then it will have to be made in another country. It is a difficult decision for me, and I am still working on finding the best solution for Shisa Brand that is both socially and environmentally sustainable, and in line with my core values. But the hand knitted line will hopefully always be made in the Faroe Islands, in limited amounts.

I really try not to give fast fashion brands my attention, as I can't possibly compete with their price points, and their mass-produced products are not comparable to my handmade garments. But there are many competitors on the Faroe Islands. Firstly there are the other knitwear brands, one of whom I actually share my shop with, but then there are the many very competent knitters who can and will easily knit their own sweater, hence not buying one of mine. To be relevant in the competition, again, the story of a Shisa Brand sweater needs to be good, and the sweater excellent. Social media has proven very important for me. It is my primary marketing tool and a very effective way to reach my current customers and followers, as well as potential customers.

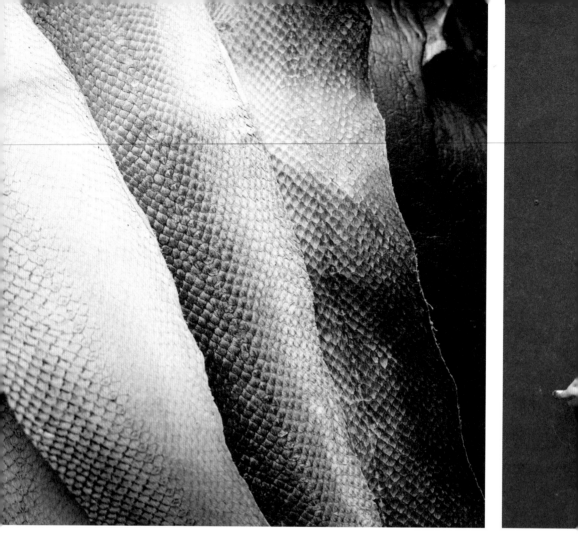

THE FUTURE

Although I aim to grow the size of Shisa Brand, size is not a goal in itself; growing in a sustainable and ethical fashion is the most important goal for me. I want to continuously create designs that "wow" customers, to create designs that last, both in terms of style and quality. Ultimately, I aim to develop designs that customers will be happy to wear for many years to come.

Besides knitting, I also work with local fish leather and seaweed fabric. In 2017 I won the Blue Fashion Challenge held on the Faroe Islands with my fish leather smock and travel bag, as well as my seal-inspired seaweed fabric dress. The main goal of the Blue Fashion Challenge was to draw attention to new ways of using a variety of marine resources, and the exciting potential there is to turn otherwise discarded bi-products and under-utilised resources into valuable, high-quality products for the fashion industry. Eleven designers from Greenland, Iceland, Faroe Islands, Denmark, Norway, Åland, and Finland were selected to compete for the prize.

I definitely see working with fish leather as part of my future. It is currently a fairly expensive fabric, but it is an interesting product with a great, highly sustainable backstory, that can be used to craft

"Ask yourself, how was this garment (or item) made, and has consideration been given to the environment and the people who made it?"

exciting products, with a beautiful texture and unique finish. I mostly use fish leather for bags and other accessories, but I believe it has huge potential for future collections. Seaweed fabrics are still in the development stages, but I really look forward to working with it in the future as it will be a very sustainable fabric that will provide designers like me with a wealth of new design possibilities.

I believe that a brand that cannot tell its sustainable story will have difficulties in the future, as the majority of consumers will demand it, along with good design, long-lasting quality, and ethical responsibility. Sustainability is going to be a currency in the fashion industry. Therefore, I think every consumer, and all craftspeople should put it into the equation now; learn to think sustainably and act accordingly. "Buy your style" is my motto, that way you don't spend money on things you won't use, nor do you unnecessarily waste the scarce resources that there are in the world. Ask yourself, how was this garment (or item) made, and has consideration been given to the environment and the people who made it?

BLOCK PRINTING

Block printing, also known as woodblock printing, is the technique of printing patterns, text, or images onto paper or textiles using a carved block of wood with inks or paints.

A mirror image of the design to be printed is hand carved from a block of wood using a variety of tools, including knives, chisels, and sandpaper. Once carved, the block is inked and repeatedly pressed against the chosen substrate to develop a repeat pattern.

- -

"The community of block printers is centuries old and has a rich history which includes the making of natural/herbal dyes, cultural and regional motifs which feature in the block prints, and the evolution of one of India's heritage crafts"

Shari Keller, Mehera Shaw

MEHERA SHAW

Shari Keller
Jaipur, India | meherashaw.com

CREATIVE BEGINNINGS

Hand block printing of textiles is one of the original indigenous crafts of Jaipur, India. Both my husband and I had close ties to that city: he was in the jewellery business and I completed my Ph.D. thesis on working with Indian artisans. With my background in textiles and my love of block-printed garments, working with the artisans in India was a natural fit.

We first developed our clothing brand, Mehera Shaw, in order to make block prints more accessible to western clothing markets. But we soon decided to manufacture our own products in to order to ensure that all fair-trade labour standards were met. The ethical aspects of production were of primary importance to us – we wanted to create a successful business but were also committed to contributing to the well-being of the artisan community. We have expanded the Mehera Shaw brand to include homewares and men's and children's clothing, as well garments for women.

> "With my background in textiles and my love of block-printed garments, working with the artisans in India was a natural fit"

MARKET RESEARCH

I would advise someone considering making a living in the craft sector to understand the full scope and needs of the supply chain and market. There are high-end, high-priced markets for craft but we have chosen to focus Mehera Shaw on everyday wear, reasonably priced.

MOTIVATION

I love every step of block printing – the alchemy of colour mixing; the block carving by hand with traditional methods; the rhythmic stamping of the block printing; the labour intensive, skilled work as the print comes to life. I love working with artisans and seeing how a myriad of traditional skills fit together to form beautiful finished products. This is slow fashion and, as such, every step matters.

> "... we make efforts to share the stories of the craft and the artisans"

We work hands-on with the artisans so sustainability takes top priority. Sustainability to me means adhering to fair-trade labour standards, the best environmental standards possible, and creating long-lasting designs. We are members of the World Fair Trade Organization and follow all labour standards. We use certified organic cottons or handloom natural fibre fabrics in all of our products, as we believe these methods support India's artisans in a more positive way as well as being more environmentally friendly. We use AZO-free dyes and have added a water filtration rain catchment system to our block printing unit to conserve and recycle water, and use traditional, artisan techniques where possible. The pros are improved sustainability in the context within which we work. The cons include the reality that slow fashion takes longer to produce and can be more expensive.

The community of block printers is centuries old and has a rich history which includes the making of natural/herbal dyes, cultural and regional motifs which feature in the block prints, and the evolution of one of India's heritage crafts. The printers themselves are highly skilled and knowledgable about their craft and the history. It is deeply inspiring to work with them, to get to know them in their community, take part in cultural events, and understand ways in which this craft has been a part of Jaipur's and Rajasthan's history for centuries. At Mehera Shaw, we make efforts to share the stories of the craft and the artisans with our customers.

I love the marriage of creativity and technique which is block printing. It is incredibly inspiring to work on projects and see them come into reality – to experience the teamwork and the happy accidents when developing new prints, colours, and styles. Our customers also value the craft and stories behind the garments. We often have long and fascinating conversations with customers who love the block prints, have travelled to visit us and other artisans, and can add stories of their own to the mix. We are all richer on a human level from this type of sharing, understanding, and appreciation. This certainly inspires a greater sense of well-being among our craftspeople and our customers.

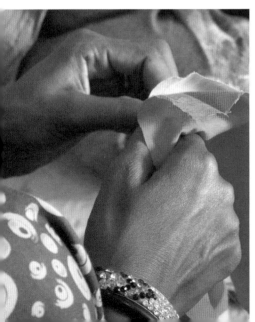

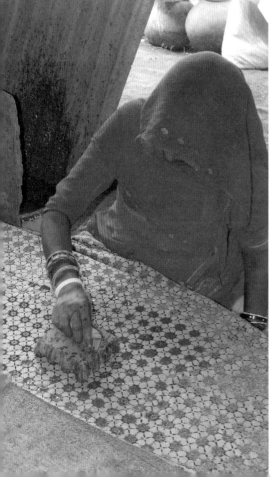

WORKSPACES

I work in many different places. I work at a messy table with hand-drawn sketches for both prints and garment styles strewn all around. My tools are mainly pencil and paper and a measuring tape. I draw all design concepts first. Garment designing for me is a very hands-on process, marrying the fabric, the shapes and colours in a harmonious blend.

At other times I work with our pattern master at his table and spend the day developing and checking on new garment styles. I also work with our master block printer out in the village checking on colours, new prints, overseeing sample printing, and checking quality. I move between all these spaces regularly.

THE DAY-TO-DAY

An average day is usually spent juggling many different aspects of the business. I write many emails to both our customers and the team, and talk with our Jaipur team daily when I am in North Carolina. I undertake many administrative tasks, such as checking spreadsheets, reviewing the workflow on our orders, checking print colours and samples, updating social media, and product catalogues, as well as taking photos. I often manage many projects and check on multiple orders throughout the day. I try and reserve certain days of the week just for quiet, creative work.

I usually work from 7.00 am to 10.00 pm, fitting in family responsibilities and kids' homework in addition to business chores. Because we sell internationally, I also try and time replies to reach different customers at appropriate times or make sure I'm available for phone calls to match my customers' work days. I spend several weeks a year in Jaipur, three or four times a year, for hands-on work with my team and with customers who visit our shop and manufacturing facilities.

I make a living through a combination of consulting work with young designers, and workshops, as well as selling wholesale and retail. We mainly sell from our Indian manufacturing site in Jaipur to customers nationally within India and internationally around the world, as well as locally from my home city in the US. We have a website and online shop and maintain a blog, Facebook, Instagram, Pinterest, LinkedIn, and Google presence. And we recently opened a flagship boutique in Jaipur, to reach both local residents and tourists interested in block printing.

Very often, crafts have untapped potential and beauty that is overlooked because they are not adjusted to suit a contemporary or western market. It is important for craft, in order to be financially sustainable, to meet the practical needs and price points customers are willing to pay. To be sustainable, craft needs to match up to high quality standards, tell the story of the process and artisans, be able to reach a market, have value, and be affordable. That's a tall order, especially when fast fashion and consumerism seem to be at all-time highs. But craft items have intrinsic value which consumers – and the fashion world – are now beginning to recognise.

BLOCK PRINTING PROCESS OVERVIEW

01 First, I design our garments and develop the print designs or concepts for each collection. I develop mood boards with images of prints, colours, motifs, and product types. I develop interesting colourways and start drawing motifs which will coordinate with the mood board. I also start sketching garment styles and define the silhouettes I'm looking for.

02 Once I have a colour palette in mind, I work with our master printer to build a range of five to ten coordinating prints for a collection. We then make fabric colour swatches and I allow the colours and feel of the prints determine the specific look and finish of the garments I design.

03 After working with the master printer to develop an effective block print design, a master carver traces the print design on to a piece of local wood.

04 Using small, sharp chisel-type tools, the master carver precisely gouges the print pattern into the block of wood.

05 After hours of highly skilled, intricate carving, the wood block is ready to use to print the fabrics.

06 The printing block is inked up and pressed down onto the fabric by hand. It is then lined up with the previous print and the printing process is repeated to cover the entire length of fabric.

07 Often, the print design contains several colours, so a new block will be made for each component of the design and will subsequently be printed in a variety of colours to create the finished print.

"Very often, crafts have untapped potential and beauty that is overlooked because they are not adjusted to suit a contemporary or western market"

KEEPING UP WITH A FAST WORLD

We have seen an increase in awareness surrounding fast fashion in recent years, especially with the introduction of Fashion Revolution Week. The global public is becoming more aware of the importance of accountability and transparency in the fashion supply chain. I believe people are also becoming more appreciative of the story behind clothing and the value of people working with others to support each other in a sustainable and respectful way.

While many of the methods we use, such as the block carving (using hand tools, rather than mechanised processes) and block printing are done in the traditional manner; the motifs, colour palettes, and garment styles are all adapted for a modern audience. We know that colours and styles, while reminiscent of, or referential to traditions, need to be updated to be wearable in the modern world, whether in India or internationally.

We are opposed to fast fashion and work on a slow fashion model in every aspect of production, from design, technique, and communication. We think that there is now a more conscious consumer that wants to invest in things with intrinsic, human-centred value and that this attitude is more in line with craft products.

"Every voice counts"

Mehera Shaw sees innovation in terms of teamwork and the human factor that stems from the fair-trade model to which we adhere. We don't see innovation as akin to a fast fashion "modernising" model. To us, innovation means using better methods of communication, working in teams, creatively recycling and upcycling materials and natural resources, and minimising waste. We strive to improve the skills of every artisan so that he or she can work most effectively and contribute to the value of our teams, helping to solve problems and innovate in ways both large and small.

Every voice counts. Our solutions and work requirements need to take into consideration the employee, including their home and family life, their cultural context and their work/life balance. Innovation can't just mean financial profit to us as a business, but the long-term sustainability of the enterprise – including everyone who works with Mehera Shaw.

"There is no such thing as more for less: "cheaper" often means someone is not getting paid a living wage and the price of that, for humanity, is very high"

Everything we make is created and done in-house – from printing the fabric, to pattern-making, sampling, stitching the garments, checking them for quality, packaging them and shipping them. We maintain a transparent positive workflow throughout the process and simply would not consider outsourcing any of this, as the teamwork is more valuable to us than any financial efficiencies. There is no such thing as more for less: "cheaper" often means someone is not getting paid a living wage and the price of that, for humanity, is very high.

Mehera Shaw is focused on making affordable products. I believe that the luxury market, even if items are made using environmentally friendly fabrics, or other sustainable materials and techniques, is not a sustainable market because it is not accessible to the average person. It seems antithetical to the concept of slow fashion to make luxury items for the wealthy instead of practical (and beautifully made) items at a reasonable price that allows people to put their money where their values are.

But there are always constraints. We have to choose our fabrics, prints, colours and garments wisely, and be ever-conscious of customer preferences, market interest, and price-points, in order to be successful. We must be dedicated to high-quality, good design, practicality and have that "something special" that sets artisan-made objects apart from the mass market. That requires discipline and the recognition that, as Dorothy Parker once said of writers, I have to "kill my darlings" – lovely but impractical designs – if we are going to meet market needs.

THE FUTURE

Our business dreams and goals are to develop our product line across a range of clothing for women, men and children, as well as homewares that make life more comfortable and beautiful. We are opening a flagship retail shop in Jaipur, and will be developing a more complete line of herbal-based dyes for our block prints. We plan for expansion of block printing workshops to develop them into an educational platform for consumers, educational institutions, and future artisans. We hope that by educating both consumers and artisans about the craft process, fair-trade production flow, and philosophy of slow fashion put into practice, we will be helping to preserve and grow both a market and artisan base for future generations.

We work continually to improve our environmental footprint. We recently improved our water filtration system to cut water use by up to 80%, are adding a rain catchment system to optimise use of seasonal rains, and plan to increase use of herbal dyes, to lessen dependence even on AZO-free chemical dyes. We also hope to switch to using more solar power and renewable energy sources, and increase our upcycling program that uses fabric scraps and other excess material for skills-training programs for women.

Consumer and industry education about the benefits – and the costs – of craft is vitally important. While the craft industry does need to meet market demands to be sustainable, knowledge about how to work with artisans effectively is also urgently needed. Craftspeople are humans, not machines. There is value in the human touch, even if – maybe because – the end product is not machine-perfect.

I believe it is not enough for customers to pressure big brands to be accountable and transparent. This simply leads to those same brands putting more pressure on factories, who generally have little capital and are working on very narrow margins, to put more pressure on their workforce. In my opinion, big brands, who are the only ones in the fashion supply chain making serious money, need to reduce CEO salaries, pay their own employees living wages, and commit to hand-in-hand, long-range financial, technological, and human resources support for their artisan-based manufacturers to increase wages and improve environmental standards.

> "... now is the time to measure quality of life not in terms of the number of garments in our closets, but in the sustainability of the world in which we live"

I'd like us to create a world in which consumers recognise the value in human productivity and creativity, appreciate the beauty of small-scale, sustainably manufactured products, and demand accountability – in terms of the environment and human dignity – from retailers, so that all can prosper and thrive. The world is recognising the price being paid for "progress" and "profitability"; now is the time to measure quality of life, not in terms of the number of garments in our closets, but in the sustainability of the world in which we live. That is the Mehera Shaw dream.

GLOSSARY

Azo-free dye

Azo dyes are one of the most commonly used types of dye used by the textile industry, and are known potential carcinogens. Azo-free dyes have not been made with the same dangerous compounds.

Bandhani

A traditional Indian method of tie-dye that involves intricately binding the textile with tiny knots.

Batt

Large thick sheet of wool.

B Corporation certified

Businesses with a B Corporation certificate meet the highest standards of social and environmental performance, public transparency, and legal accountability.

Beater

A weaving tool used to push the weft yarn securely into place on the loom.

Carder

Carding is the process of brushing wool fibres to create a neat web of fibres, ready to be used in a range of different forms. Wool can be processed using a handheld carder or using a larger mechanical drum carder, depending on the quantity that needs to be brushed.

Cochineal

Also known as "carmine", cochineal is a scarlet dye derived from the crushed dried bodies of scale insects.

Closed-loop system

A circular system that ensures no waste and utilises reuse to get the most out of a product or garment.

Colourfast

Dyed colours that will not fade or be washed out.

Cut, make, trim (CMT)

The term used for the garment-making service a factory can offer. Using a design, a factory will cut the pattern pieces, assemble the garment and finish it with the required trimmings.

Direct warping

The high-speed process of adding warp threads to a loom. It is often used for making fabric of a single colour.

Drop spindle

A tool used to spin fibres into yarn. It is often the first step before using the yarn on a spinning wheel.

Dyestuff

A substance that can be used as a dye.

End-of-line fabrics

Fabrics that are no longer in production. Often heavily discounted as they often cannot be purchased in high quantities.

Fibershed

A project in California that works to develop regenerative regional fibre systems for independent producers to rebuild regional manufacturing to craft biodegradable products that in turn, reduce ecological footprint.

Fish leather

Leather made from the fish skin discarded by the seafood industry.

Grainline

Grain refers to the orientation of the weft and warp threads. A grainline is the line that the warp follows.

Greenwashing

Using misleading green marketing to make a company or product appear to be more environmentally friendly that it really is.

Hapa zome

The Japanese art of hammering leaves, flowers, and other organic matter into a substrate to create natural prints.

Heddle

A fundamental component of a loom. To separate the warp threads and prepare them for weaving of the weft, each warp thread is passed through a heddle.

Hem

A method of finishing the edges of cloth. The cloth is first folded and then sewn, to prevent fraying.

Ikat

A traditional Indonesian dyeing technique which involves resist dyeing yarn before weaving into cloth.

Indigo

A rich dark blue dye derived from the indigo plant, a tropical plant of the pea family.

Lazy Kate

A tool used during yarn spinning that holds one or more spools while the yarn is wound off them.

Linen

A hard-wearing and breathable textile made from the fibres of the flax plant.

Loom

A piece of apparatus used to weave yarn into fabric. Looms can come in mechanised form or small hand form.

Merino wool

Wool taken from the Merino breed of sheep is incredibly soft and fine, as well as naturally long and strong.

Mordant

A fixative substance that is used to aid the absorption of dye into fabric.

Niddy-Noddy

A tool that is used to make skeins of yarn. It is made up of a central bar, with crossbars at each end, at 90-degree angles from one another.

Notions

Small tools or objects used in sewing. Notions could include items to finish a garment, such as buttons, or tools such as pins or seam rippers.

Overlocker

A specialised sewing machine that sews over several pieces of cloth. Often used for hemming or seaming a garment.

Reed

A component of the weaving loom, a reed resembles a comb and is used to separate the warp threads, guide the motion of the shuttle across the loom, and to align the weft threads into place.

Rolag

A roll of fibres used to spin woollen yarn.

rPET

Recycled polyethylene terephthalate. In it's virgin state, polyethylene terephthalate is used to make a variety of different products, such as bottles and packaging.

Running stitch
A simple stitch that consists of a line of even stitches which run through the cloth without overlapping.

Sashiko
A form of repair that enhances a worn or damaged element of a garment and celebrates its imperfections.

Sewing pattern
Paper templates for the individual components of a dressmaking design.

Shuttle
An integral part of the weaving loom, the shuttle carries the thread of the weft yarn, and during weaving, it passes back and forth through the loom to weave the weft yarn between the warp thread to create cloth.

Skein
Thread or yarn that has been loosely coiled and knotted, ready to use in weaving, sewing, or knitting.

Soil-to-soil
A regenerative method of working that aims to only create natural products that can be safely re-entered into the earth once their useful life ends. For example, a biodegradable material such as wool can be returned to the soil after its use.

Spinning wheel
Apparatus used for spinning thread from raw fibres.

Swift
A wooden tool used to hold yarn while it is being wound off the spool. With an adjustable diameter, the umbrella-like contraption can hold skeins of yarns of many lengths, and rotates around a central rod.

Toile
A type of translucent linen or cotton fabric. The term "toile" can also be used to refer to an early sample garment, created to test a dressmaking pattern.

Treadle
A lever worked by foot to operate a machine.

Upcycle
Also known as "creative reuse", upcycling utilises existing materials to create something new and useful.

Warp and weft
The two basic constituents of fabric. Longitudinal yarns, known as the warp, are woven with latitudinal yarns, known as the weft, to create the basis of all textiles.

Woodblocks
Printing blocks that are intricately carved from wood and used to create repeat patterns on fabric and paper.

Wool comb
A comb designed to be used to brush out the organic debris from raw wool before processing it further using carders.

Yarn
Thread that has been spun onto a reel.

Zero waste
Employing a set of principles that focus on waste prevention and aim to eliminate waste through recycling and reusing production methods.

"... balancing rich textures in the weft and an openness in the warp creates drape and depth in the finished works"

Imogen Di Sapia,

Bright Moon Weaving Studio

FURTHER READING & RESOURCES

Fashion Revolution
fashionrevolution.org

Ellen McArthur Foundation
ellenmacarthurfoundation.org

Reverse Resources
reverseresources.net

Stop Micro Waste
stopmicrowaste.com

Other Biological Futures, Alexandra Daisy Ginsberg and Natsai Chieza
jods.mitpress.mit.edu/pub/issue4-ginsberg-chieza

Bridget Harvey
bridgetharvey.co.uk

Bristol Cloth
bristolcloth.co.uk

Bristol Weaving Mill
bristolweavingmill.co.uk

Fibershed
fibershed.com

Green Fashion Tours, Berlin
greenfashiontours.com

Client Earth
clientearth.org

Faye Toogood
fayetoogood.com

Blue Fashion Challenge
nora.fo/blue-fashion-challenge
jonaa.org/content/2017/10/12/blue-fashion-challenge

Zenana Women
zenanawomen.com.au/index.php/stories/aboutus

Mayamiko Trust
mayamiko.org

World Fair Trade Organization
wfto.com

END NOTES

Introduction: A creative future

1 and 2 *A New Textiles Economy: Redesigning Fashion's Future*, Ellen McArthur Foundation, 2017

3 *National Overview: Facts and Figures on Materials, Wastes and Recycling*, United States Environmental Protection Agency (EPA), www.epa.gov

4 *Creating a Digitally Enhanced Circular Economy*, Reverse Resources, 2017

5 *The 2018 Apparel Industry Overproduction Report and Infographic*, Sharecloth.com, 2018

6 stopmicrowaste.com

ACKNOWLEDGEMENTS

OPENING PAGES
p. 3 © Miquel Llonch
p. 4 © Proudly Made in Africa
p. 6 © Beinta á Torkilsheyggi
p. 8 © Deva O'Neill

FOREWORD
p. 10 (top left), 12 © Boy Kloves
p. 10 (middle right), 13 (bottom) © Jelly Luise
p. 10 (all photos except middle right), 13 (top)
© Cindy Sasha

INTRODUCTION
p. 14, 16-17 © Ian Delú for Fashion Revolution
Germany
p. 19 © Cherie Birkner
p. 21 © 3dtotal.com Ltd
p. 22 © Beinta á Torkilsheyggi
p. 24 © Ben Mönks
p. 25 © Christopher Ross
p. 26 © Proudly Made in Africa
p. 27 © Fidelis Fuchs

BOTANICAL DYEING
p. 28-44 All photos © 3dtotal.com Ltd
p. 46, 52-53, 59 (top right) © Kestrel Jenkins
(@kestrelee) and Drew McGill (@drewfoto) of
Falcon Related (@falconrelated)
p. 49 © Kestrel Jenkins (@kestrelee) and
Drew McGill (@drewfoto) of Falcon Related
(@falconrelated) modelled by Britt Rafuson
p. 50, 51 (bottom right), 56-57, 59 (top

left), 60 (bottom), 61 © Kestrel Jenkins (@
kestrelee) and Drew McGill (@drewfoto) of
Falcon Related (@falconrelated) modelled
by Natalie Boras of NewMARK Models
(@newmarkmodels), make-up by Jessica
Tyransky (@jt_hairandmakeup), jewellery by
Eliza Sloane (@elizasloanejewelry)
p. 60 (top right) © Chelsea Francis, modelled
by Gia

All other photos © Nicki Patel

UPCYCLING
p. 62-77 All photos © Ben Mönks
p. 86 (top right), 89 © Olivier Valiente
p. 88 © Blixt

All other photos © demano

WEAVING
p. 90-107 All photos © Amy Very
p. 108, 112-115, 116 (top) 119 (bottom), 121 ©
Janelle Jones
p. 111, 116 (bottom), 119 (top), 120 © Summer
Moore
p. 121, 125 (top left), 127-129, 132-133, 136-137 ©
Miquel Llonch
p.125 (bottom, top right), 131, 135 © Roke
p. 138, 141- 142, 144-149 (images 01-06) 150, 151
(bottom), 152 (bottom right), 155 (top left) ©
Christopher Ross
p. 143, 149 (image 07), 152 (all except bottom

right), 155 (all except top left) © David Ross
p. 151 (top) © Pragya Singh

SHOEMAKING
Juta Shoes
p. 156-169 All photos © Kanahaya Alam

GARMENT MAKING
p. 170-183 All photos © Deva O'Neill
p. 184, 188 (top), 189 (bottom), 194 (top), 197
(top left, bottom) © Sebastien Genet (@
sebastiengenetphotography)
p. 189 (top), 190 (bottom), 194 (bottom), 197 (top
right) © Action Wolf Media
p. 193 © Punchline Media (@punchline_
media)
p. 198, 201, 203 (all except bottom), 207 (image
07) © Munjiri
p. 203 (bottom), 208-211 © Wolf and Badger
Studios
p. 204 (bottom, top right) 205 © Just Glow
p. 204 (top left), 207 (image 06) © Proudly
Made in Africa

All other photos © Mayamiko

MENDING
p. 212, 218-219, photos and tutorial by
Katrina Rodabaugh first appeared in Taproot
Magazine Issue 30: Feast
p. 217, 221, 224-245 © Karen Pearson

p. 214, 222 © Katrina Rodabaugh

FELT MAKING
p. 226-245 all photos © Tali Kimelman, art
direction by Valentina León and Alice Otegui

KNITTING
p. 251 (bottom), 259 (top) © Klara Johannesen
p. 260-261 © Karen Sissal Kjartansdóttir
Kristiansen

All other photos © Beinta á Torkilsheyggi

BLOCK PRINTING
p. 263-264, 270-271 (images 01, 04), 275 (top) ©
Mehera Shaw Textiles Pvt. Ltd.
p. 262, 267-268, 270-271 (images 02, 03, 05, 06,
07), 272-273, 275 (bottom) © Shari Keller

GLOSSARY
p. 276 © 3dtotal.com Ltd
p. 279 © David Ross
p. 280 © Amy Very

FURTHER READING
& RESOURCES
p. 282 © Tali Kimelman, art direction by
Valentina León and Alice Otegui

"Crafts demonstrate our heritage and our history, and are something to be respected, preserved, admired, and shared with the world"

Babs Behan, Botanical Inks

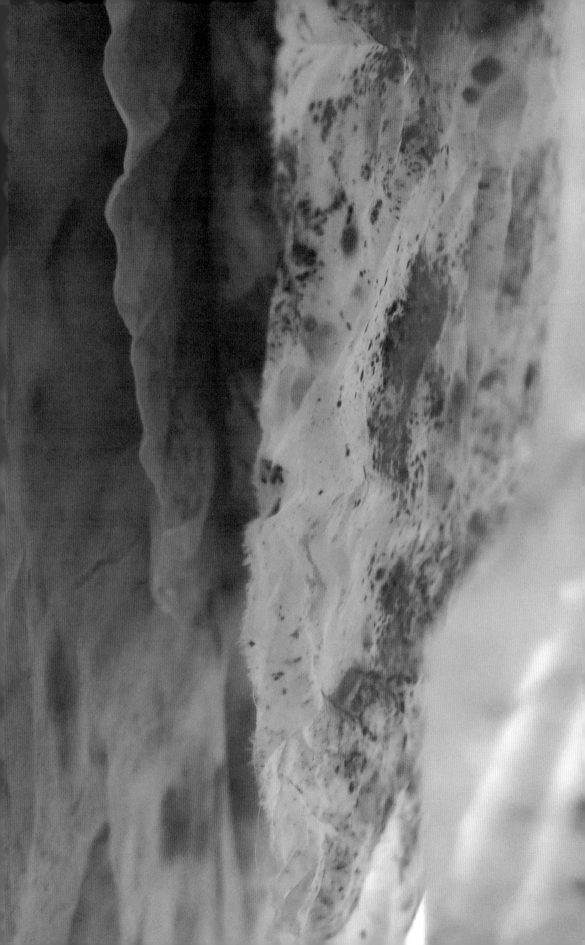

THE SEARCH FOR WELL-BEING AND SUSTAINABILITY IN THE MODERN WORLD

An imprint of 3dtotal Publishing, Canopy Press was established in 2018 to create books focused on traditional crafts, lifestyle, and the environment. With an interest in enjoying the simple things in life, Canopy Press aims to build awareness around sustainable living, a mindful approach to arts and crafts, and an appreciation of the earth we dwell on.

Marrying great aesthetics with enlightening stories from real people, our *Search for Well-being and Sustainability in the Modern World* series presents an insight into heritage crafts and artisan food, and their revival and survival in the modern world. Visit our website and follow us on Instagram to stay up to date with forthcoming books and news.

canopy-press.com | instagram.com/canopypress